IQALUIT ᐃᖃᓗᐃᑦ

PHOTOGRAPHY AND TEXT BY NICK NEWBERY ᐊᔾᔨᓕᐅᖅᑎ ᐊᒻᒪ ᑎᑎᕋᖅᑎ ᓂᒃ ᓂᐅᐱᐅᕆ PHOTOGRAPHIE ET TEXTE DE NICK NEWBERY

Iqaluit

Photography and text by Nick Newbery

© Photography and text Nick Newbery, 2009

All rights reserved. No part of this publication may be reproduced in any manner or method without written permission from the publisher, except by a reviewer who wishes to quote brief passages and include a few photographs in a review.

First Edition 1995, Second Edition 1999,
Third Edition 2009

Library and Archives Canada Cataloguing in Publication

Newbery, Nick, 1944-
Iqaluit / photography and text by Nick Newbery = photographie et texte de Nick Newbery. -- 3rd ed.

Text in English, Inuktitut (in syllabic characters) and French. Co-published by: Royal Canadian Legion, no. 168, Iqaluit.
ISBN 978-1-55036-800-0

1. Iqaluit (Nunavut)--Pictorial works. 2. Iqaluit (Nunavut)--History.
I. Royal Canadian Legion. Branch no. 168, Iqaluit
II. Title.

FC4346.37.N49 2009 917.19'500222
C2009-904338-6E

Cover photo: Eliyah and Annie Nauyuk

Endpapers: Frobisher Bay, NT, 1957
Margaret Burton with permission.

Jacket, cover and book design by Nortext

Printed and bound in Canada

Published for the Royal Canadian Legion Branch No. 168, Iqaluit
by Nortext Publishing Corporation

Nortext Publishing Corporation
P.O. Box 8
Iqaluit NU X0A 0H0
Canada

ᐃᖃᓗᐃᑦ

ᐊᔾᔨᓕᐅᖅᑎ ᐊᒻᒪ ᑎᑎᕋᖅᑎ ᓂᒃ ᓂᐅᐱᐅᕆ

© ᐊᔾᔨᓕᐅᖅᑎ ᐊᒻᒪ ᑎᑎᕋᖅᑎ ᓂᒃ ᓂᐅᐱᐅᕆ, 2009

ᐃᓱᓐᓇᑎᒃ ᐱᔪᙳᓇᐅᑎᑦ ᐱᓯᒪᔭᐅᔪᑦ. ᓯᓈᑐᐃᓐᓇᖓ ᑖᒃᓯᒪ ᐅᖃᓕᒫᓕᐊᖑᓯᒪᔪᑉ ᓴᓇᔭᐅᒃᑳᓂᖏᐊᖃᙱᑦᑐᖅ ᖃᓄᐃᑦᑐᑐᐃᓐᓇᐅᓗᒍ ᐅᕝᕙᓘᓐᓃᑦ ᖃᓄᑐᐃᓐᓇᖅ ᐊᖏᖅᑕᐅᓯᒪᙱᑦᑐᓂ ᐅᖃᓕᒫᓕᐅᖅᑎᓂᑦ, ᐊᔪᕆᑎᑕᐅᔪᑐᐊᑦ ᑕᑯᒋᐊᒃᑲᓂᖅᑎᐅᔪᑦ ᐊᐅᓚᔾᔭᓐᓂᖅᑐᓂᒃ ᓇᐃᑦᑐᓂᒃ ᐅᖃᐅᓯᕐᓂᒃ ᐊᑐᕈᒪᔪᑦ ᐊᒻᒪ ᐃᓚᓯᖕᓂᒡᓗᑎᒃ ᐊᒥᔫᖏᑦᑐᓂᒃ ᐊᔾᔨᓂᒃ ᑕᑯᒋᐊᒃᑲᓂᕐᓂᒥ.

ᓯᕗᓪᓕᖅᐹᖅ ᓴᖅᑭᑕᐅᓂᖓ 1995, ᑭᖑᓪᓕᖅ ᓴᖅᑭᑕᐅᓂᖓ 1999,
ᐱᖓᔪᖓᑦ ᓴᖅᑭᑕᐅᓂᖓ 2009

ᑲᓇᑕᒥ ᑎᑎᖅᑲᑕᐅᓯᒪᓂᖓ ᐅᖃᓕᒫᓕᐊᖑᔪᓂᒃ ᓇᓂᓯᔾᔪᑎᓂ

Newbery, Nick, 1944-
Iqaluit / photography and text by Nick Newbery = photographie et texte de Nick Newbery. -- 3rd ed.

Text in English, Inuktitut (in syllabic characters) and French. Co-published by: Royal Canadian Legion, no. 168, Iqaluit.
ISBN 978-1-55036-800-0

1. Iqaluit (Nunavut)--Pictorial works. 2. Iqaluit (Nunavut)--History.
I. Royal Canadian Legion. Branch no. 168, Iqaluit
II. Title.

FC4346.37.N49 2009 917.19'500222
C2009-904338-6E

ᖄᖓᒍᑦ ᐊᔾᔨᙳᐊᖅ: ᐃᓚᐃᔭ ᐊᒻᒪᓗ ᐋᓂ ᓇᐅᔪᖅ

ᐃᓱᐊᓂ ᐸᐃᑉᐹᑦ: ᐳᕿᔅᐱᓯᖅ ᐸᐃ, ᓄᓇᑦᓯᐊᖅ 1957
ᒫᒍᓚᑦ ᐆᖅᑕᓐ ᐊᖏᖅᑕᐅᓯᒪᔫᑦᑐᓂ.

ᐅᓕᕆᔭᖓ, ᖃᖓ ᐊᒻᒪ ᐅᖃᓕᒫᑉ ᓴᓇᓯᒪᓂᖓ ᐋᖅᑭᒃᓯᖅᑕᐅᔪᖅ ᓄᐊᑕᒃᓯᒥᑦ

ᑎᑎᖅᑕᐅᔪᖅ ᐊᒻᒪ ᑲᑎᑕᐅᑦᑐᓂ ᑲᓇᑕᒥ

ᕿᐃᐅᑦ ᑲᓇᐃᑎᐊᓐ ᓖᔾᔭᓐ
ᓇᒻᒪ 168, ᐃᖃᓗᐃᑦ
ᓴᓇᔭᐅᔪᖅ ᓄᐊᑕᒃᓯ ᐅᖃᓕᒫᒐᒃᓴᓕᐅᖅᑎᓂᑦ

Nortext Publishing Corporation
P.O. Box 8
Iqaluit NU X0A 0H0
Canada

Iqaluit

Photographies et texte de Nick Newbery

© Photographies et texte de Nick Newbery, 2009

Tous droits réservés. Aucune partie de cette publication ne peut être reproduite de quelque façon que ce soit sans une autorisation écrite de l'éditeur, sauf de brèves citations avec photos dans le cadre d'une critique.

Première édition 1995, Deuxième édition 1999,
Troisième édition 2009

Catalogage avant publication de Bibliothèque et Archives Canada

Newbery, Nick, 1944-
Iqaluit / photography and text by Nick Newbery = photographie et texte de Nick Newbery. -- 3e éd.

Texte en anglais, en inuktitut (alphabet syllabique) et en français. Publ. en collab. avec: Légion royale canadienne, Filiale Iqaluit no 168.
ISBN 978-1-55036-800-0

1. Iqaluit (Nunavut)--Ouvrages illustrés. 2. Iqaluit (Nunavut)--Histoire.
I. Légion royale canadienne. Filiale Iqaluit no 168
II. Titre.

FC4346.37.N49 2009 917.19'500222
C2009-904338-6F

Photo en couverture : Eliyah et Annie Nauyuk

Feuilles de garde : Frobisher Bay, NT, 1957
Avec la permission de Margaret Burton.

Conception de la jaquette, de la couverture et du livre par Nortext.

Imprimé et relié au Canada.

Publié pour la Légion royale canadienne
Section locale Iqaluit n° 168, Iqaluit
par Nortext Publishing Corporation.

Nortext Publishing Corporation
Case postale 8
Iqaluit NU X0A 0H0
Canada

IQALUIT ᐃᖃᓗᐃᑦ

PHOTOGRAPHY AND TEXT BY NICK NEWBERY　　ᐊᕐᓇᑐᐅᖅᑎ ᐊᒻᒪ ᑎᑎᕋᖅᑎ ᓂᒃ ᓄᐅᐱᐅᕆ　　PHOTOGRAPHIE ET TEXTE DE NICK NEWBERY

THE ROYAL CANADIAN LEGION

Due to the success of its first two coffee table books on Iqaluit, the executive of the local branch of the Royal Canadian Legion decided to release a third edition of its 1995 publication. This trilingual issue has become a popular staple with residents and visitors alike, capturing tradition and change not only in Iqaluit but throughout the Eastern Arctic. By issuing an updated version of this Canadian best-seller by long-time northerner Nick Newbery it was felt that readers could continue to enjoy a taste of Nunavut's capital set amid glimpses of the history, the people and the territory that it represents.

The Executive and Members
The Royal Canadian Legion
Branch No.168
Iqaluit, Nunavut

October 2009

Chris Groves
President

ᑲᔪᓯᑦᑎᐊᖅᓯᒪᓂᖏᓐᓄᑦ ᓯᕗᓪᓕᖅᐹᒃ ᒪᕐᕿᒃ ᑭᐳᒥᐅᑕᑦ ᖀᒥᕐᕿᐊᓖᒃ ᐱᔾᔪᑎᖃᖅᑐᑦ ᐃᖃᓗᐃᑦ, ᕿᐃᔪᓪ ᑲᓇᑎᐊᓐ ᓈᔾᖑᑦ ᐊᐅᓚᑦᑎᔨᖏᑦ ᓄᓇᓕᖓᓂ ᐱᓕᕆᐊ ᓴᖅᑭᑦᑎᒃᑲᓐᓂᕋᓯᓪᓕᖅᓯᒪᕗᑦ ᐱᖓᔪᐃᓪᓕᖅᑕᖓᓂᒃ ᐅᖃᓪᓚᒫᒐᒥᒃ 1995-ᒥ ᓴᖅᑭᑕᐅᓯᒪᔪᒥᒃ. ᑖᓐᓇ ᐱᖓᓱᓪᓕᖅᑲᖓᔪᑎᒍᑦ ᐅᖃᐅᓯᓪᓚᒃ ᓴᖅᑭᑕᐅᓯᒪᔪᖅ ᐊᑐᓂ ᓄᓇᖃᖅᑎᐅᔪᓄᑦ ᐳᓛᓂᐊᖅᓯᒪᔪᓄᑦ ᐱᐅᕆᔪᐅᒪᓇᓪᓕᖅᓯᒪᓪᓗᓂ, ᑕᑯᒃᓴᐅᓂᖃᖅᑎᑦᑎᓪᓗᓂ ᐃᓪᓕᖅᑯᓯᑐᖃᖕᔪᐅᔪᒥᒃ ᐊᓯᔾᔨᖅᐸᓪᓕᐊᓂᐅᔪᒥᓪᓗ ᐃᖃᓗᓐᓂᑐᐊᖑᖏᑦᑐᖅ ᑭᓯᐊᓂᑦᑕᐅᖅ ᐅᑭᐅᖅᑕᖅᑑᑉ ᑲᓇᖕᓇᓖᖓᓂ. ᓴᖅᑭᑕᐅᓗᓂ ᓄᑖᕈᓇᐊᖅᓯᒪᔪᖅ ᐅᓂᒃᑳᓕᐊᖑᔪᒪᓂᖓ ᑖᓐᓇ ᑲᓇᑕᒥ ᐱᐅᕆᔭᐅᓂᖅᐹᖑᓪᓗᓂ ᓂᐅᕕᐊᒃᓴᓇᔭᐅᓯᒪᔪᖅ ᐊᑯᓂᐅᓪᓚᖅᑐᒧᑦ ᐅᑭᐅᖅᑕᖅᑐᕐᒥᐅᑕᐅᓯᒪᓪᓚᖅᑐᒧᑦ ᓂᒃ ᓂᐅᐱᐅᓇ ᐃᒃᐱᕆᔭᐅᓯᒪᖕᒪᑦ ᐅᖃᓖᖅᑎᐅᔭᑦ ᖁᕕᐊᕆᔭᖃᐃᓐᓇᕈᓐᓇᕐᓂᐊᕐᓗᑎᒃ ᖃᓄᐃᑦᑑᓚᓇᒻᒪᖔᑦ ᓄᓇᕗᑦ ᐊᖓᔪᖄᖄᕕᐊᑕ ᖃᓄᐃᓕᐊᓐᖓᕈᑎᕆᓯᒪᔭᖏᓐᓂᒃ, ᐃᓄᖁᑎᖏᓐᓂᒃ ᐊᒻᒪᓗ ᐊᕕᒃᑐᖅᓯᒪᓂᐊᓐᓂᑦᑐᕐᖁᑎᖓᓂᒃ ᑭᒡᓕᖅᑐᖅᑕᖏᑦ.

ᐊᐅᓚᑦᑎᔨ ᐃᓚᒥᔭᐅᔪᓪᓗ
ᕿᐃᔪᓪ ᑲᓇᑎᐊᓐ ᓈᔾᓐ
ᐊᒡᒍᖅᑐᖅᓯᒪᓂᐊᑕ ᓈᓴᐅᑖ 168
ᐃᖃᓗᐃᑦ, ᓄᓇᕗᑦ
ᐅᑐᐱᕆ 2009

ᑯᕆᔅ ᒍᕉᕝᔅ
ᐊᖓᔪᖄᖅ

Michel Albert / ᒥᓯᐅᓪ ᐃᐅᓪᐳᑦ

Devant le succès qu'ont connu ses deux premiers beaux livres grand format sur Iqaluit, la direction du bureau local de la Légion royale canadienne a décidé de publier la troisième édition de son ouvrage de 1995. Cette édition trilingue connaît une grande popularité auprès des résidents et des visiteurs, faisant valoir la tradition et les changements propres à Iqaluit, mais aussi dans l'ensemble de l'est de l'Arctique. En publiant une version mise à jour de ce best-seller canadien de ce citoyen de longue date du Nord, Nick Newbery, on pressentait que les lecteurs pourraient continuer d'apprécier la découverte du caractère unique de la capitale du Nunavut, agrémentée d'un regard sur l'histoire, les gens et le territoire qu'elle représente.

La direction et les membres
Légion royale canadienne
Bureau n° 168
Iqaluit, Nunavut

Octobre 2009

Chris Groves
Président

Introduction

Iqaluit, the capital of Canada's newest territory, Nunavut, is only a three-hour jet flight from Ottawa or Montreal but the civilisation that the traveller steps into upon arrival in the North is a world away from the hustle and bustle which is so often a part of life in the South.

For most Canadians, Iqaluit's significance lies in its being the seat of government for the Canadian Eastern Arctic. For others, it is perhaps the gateway to Nunavut, to the gentler pace of the small, closely-knit Inuit communities or to several unique national and territorial parks. For still others, both Inuit and *Qallunaat* (non-Inuit), Iqaluit is simply the place to call home, offering a rendez-vous for Inuit, French and English cultures and a milieu where tradition and technology can successfully blend on a daily basis.

The creation of a new Arctic territory called Nunavut in 1999 changed the map of Canada and, by becoming the capital of that territory, Iqaluit changed too, seeing a large increase in its population, in local employment and in its economy. It is no longer some remote outpost of a colonial administration. It has become the centre of government for the Eastern Arctic and as such has stepped into a brave new

ᐱᒋᐊᕐᓂᖅ

ᐃᖃᓗᐃᑦ, ᑲᓇᑕᐅᑉ ᓄᑕᐅᓂᖅᐹᖑᒻᒪᑕ ᐊᕕᒃᑐᖅᓯᒪᓂᐊᓄ ᐊᕐᕕᒃᓯᒃᕿᖓᑦ, ᓄᓇᕗᑦ, ᐱᖓᓱᑦ-ᐃᒃᕿᖏᒡ ᐳᕐᑐᒃ ᖃᖓᑕᒥᒃ ᐊᑐᓄᖅᑲᔾᐃᐊᒍᓯᖅ ᐊᒍᑦᓯᒃ ᒪᓐᑐᔨᐊᒥᓘᓐᓃᑦ ᑭᓯᐊᓂ ᐃᓄᐃᑦ ᐃᓯᕐᕿᖅᑭᑐᓄ ᑎᑭᑦᑕᖅᓯᒡᒥᒃ ᐅᐱᕐᖃᑦᓴᒥᒍᑐᒐ ᓄᓇᕐᕿᑎᒐ ᐅᖃᕝᐸᐅᖅᓂᓐᖅ ᔪᐊᓐᐃᓇᒍᖅᕿᑐᒡᓂᒃ ᑕᐃᒪ ᖃᓄᖃᖅᓂᕐᐃᒍ ᐃᓘᕐᒧᐅ-ᒪᑉᐹᕐᖅᓯᒃ.

ᑕᒪᕐᒥᒍᑐ ᑲᓇᒥᕐᑎᐅᑕᒡ, ᐃᓄᐃᑦ ᐱᖕᒪᐅᑎᕐᒪᕐᑖᕐᑦ ᐃᓇᖁᒡᐃᖅᐸᖅ ᓴᕐᒐᑦᑎᖓᒍᐱᒡ ᑲᓇᑕᐅᑉ ᐅᐱᕐᖃᖅᑐᖓᑦ ᑲᖃᖃᕿᓂᒡ. ᐊᑐᕐᕿᒐᒡ, ᐃᓘᕐᖅ ᒐᐅᓴᑦᒥᐅᕐᒃᖃᕕᓂᒐ ᓄᓇᖁᒡ, ᖃᐅᐃᑕᕐᐅᒐᕿᔪᖕᒃᑐᒐᑦ ᐱᕐᖃᖑᖕᒃᑐᒡᒃ ᒥᒃᑕᒥᒡ, ᐃᓯᕐᖃᖕᒃᑎᑦᑐᒐ ᐃᓄᐃᑦ ᓄᐊᒐᕐᒃ ᐅᕐᕿᒐ ᐊᕐᒐᓕᐴᕐᖑᒡ ᐊᕐᓴᐅᕐᐃᑦᔪᒡ ᑲᓇᒥ ᐊᑕᐅᑦᑐᖅᖁᖓᐴᕐᖁᑐᒐ ᒥᕐᖃᓗᐊᒃᑎᖅᕼᐅᕿ. ᑭᓐ ᐊᑐᕐᕿᒐ, ᐊᒍᐊ ᐃᐳᒃᑦ ᖃᖅᓴᓂᒃ, ᐃᖃᓗᐃᑦ ᐊᕐᕐᖏᖅᕐᒃᑐᒐᐃᐊᓇᒥᒡ, ᑭᓐᕼᕃᐊᐃᑦᑎᖕᒐ ᐃᓇᖓᓄᒡ, ᐳᐃᕿᓇᒡ ᖃᓇᒥᕿᓂᒡ ᐊᔪᒐ ᐊᖅᐸᒃᓇᒍᒐᖕᒃ ᐃᓇᕿᑯᐱᐃᔨᒐᒃᐳᖅᓇᒐ ᓄᑲᓇᐴᕐᖃᒃᖃᖅ-ᐴᕃᓇᕿᑐᒡ ᑲᕐᒐᕿᖕᒐᐴᕃᕃᕐᔪᒡ ᑲᒥᑕᐴᒐᐱᐳᒐᒍᑦ ᖃᕿᑕᒃᓂᕼᐅᔨᒐᓇᕿᓂᒡ.

Introduction

Iqaluit, capitale du plus récent territoire canadien, le Nunavut, n'est qu'à trois heures d'Ottawa ou de Montréal, à vol d'oiseau, mais la civilisation que le voyageur découvre à son arrivée dans le Nord est à mille lieues de la vie frénétique qui caractérise si souvent les régions du Sud.

Pour la plupart des Canadiens, l'importance d'Iqaluit tient au fait qu'elle est le siège du gouvernement de l'est de l'Arctique canadien. Pour d'autres, elle est la porte d'entrée du Nunavut, au rythme de vie plus calme des petites communautés très unies ou des nombreux parcs territoriaux et nationaux uniques de la région. Pour d'autres encore, Inuits et *Qallunaat* (non-Inuits), Iqaluit est simplement leur ville de résidence, point de rencontre des cultures inuite, française et anglaise, et milieu où la tradition et la technologie se côtoient avec bonheur jour après jour.

La création d'un nouveau territoire arctique appelé Nunavut en 1999 a changé la carte du Canada et, en devenant la capitale de ce territoire, Iqaluit s'est également transformée, sa population, les emplois locaux et son économie connaissant une croissance importante. Ce n'est plus un

world, from hosting international leaders to dealing with the impact of issues created in far-away places.

Despite forming one fifth of the land mass of Canada, Nunavut has a small population (31,000 in 2009), which gives it the feeling of a somewhat large, over-extended family. In Iqaluit, where political leaders can be met on the streets and in the stores on a daily basis, government often comes wrapped in the flavour of small-town friendliness, a situation that can sometimes work to the advantage of its citizens!

Early days

The land on which the city now stands was not heavily used by Inuit prior to the building of a permanent community because for centuries people had preferred to live in small, widely-distributed camps around Frobisher Bay.

ᐱᓐᖑᖅᑎᑕᐅᓯᒪᓂᖓ ᓄᑖᖅ ᐅᑭᐅᖅᑕᖅᑐᒥ ᐊᕕᒃᑐᖅᓯᒪᓂᐊ ᑕᐃᔭᐅᓪᓗᓂ ᓄᓇᕗᑦ 1999-ᒥ ᑲᓇᑕᐅᑉ ᓄᓇᙳᐊᓇᔭᖓᓄᑦ ᐊᓯᔾᔨᓯᒪᔪᖅ ᐊᒻᒪᓗ, ᑖᔅᓱᒪ ᐊᕕᒃᑐᖅᓯᒪᓂᐊᓃᑦᑐᒥ ᐊᖓᔪᖅᑳᖅᑲᕐᕕᐅᓕᖅᓯᒪᓪᓗᓂ, ᐃᖅᑲᓗᐃᑦᑕᐅᖅ ᐊᓯᔾᔨᖅᓯᒪᓕᓇᒍᖅ, ᑕᒡᒐᓗ ᐊᒥᓯᑭᖅᓯᒪᓕᕐᓂᖏᓐᓄᑦ ᐃᓄᐃᑦ ᐊᒥᓲᓂᖏᑦ, ᓄᓇᓕᖓᓂ ᐃᖅᑲᓇᐃᔫᖅᑲᕐᓂᐅᔪᓂᒃ ᐊᒻᒪᓗ ᒪᑭᒪᐅᑎᖏᓐᓄᑦ. ᐅᖓᓯᒃᑐᕐᒥᐅᑕᐅᔪᓐᓃᕐᓯᒪᓂᖅᑲᖅᐳᑦ ᐊᐅᓚᑦᑎᕕᐅᓕᖅᓯᒪᓂᖓᓄᑦ. ᑐᓐᖓᕕᓪᓗᐊᑕᐅᓕᖅᓯᒪᔪᖅ ᑲᑐᒪᖅᑲᕐᕕᐅᓂᖓᓂᒃ ᐅᑭᐅᖅᑕᖅᑑᑉ ᑲᓇᖕᓇᖓᓄᑦ ᐊᒻᒪᓗ ᑕᐃᒪᐃᓐᓂᖓᓄᑦ ᑎᑭᐅᑎᓯᒪᓪᓗᓂ ᓴᐱᖏᓐᓂᖅᑳᑦᑎᐊᕐᑐᒧᑦ ᓄᑖᒧᑦ ᓄᓇᕐᔪᐊᖑᓕᖅᓯᒪᔪᒧᑦ, ᑐᓐᖓᓱᒃᑎᑦᑎᔨᐅᓯᒪᓪᓗᓂ ᓄᓇᕐᔪᐊᒥ ᓯᕗᓕᖅᑎᐅᔪᓂᑦ ᑎᑭᓪᓗᒍ ᐱᓕᕆᐊᖅᑳᕐᓂᕐᒧᑦ ᐊᒃᑐᐃᔭᐅᓯᒪᓂᐅᔪᓄᑦ ᐱᔾᔪᑎᒃᓴᐅᔪᓂᒃ ᓴᖅᑭᑕᐅᓯᒪᔪᑦ ᐅᖓᓯᒃᑐᒻᒪᕆᐅᔪᓂᑦ ᓄᓇᓕᐅᔪᓂ.

ᑲᓇᑕᒥ ᐊᕙᐅᑉ ᐅᖓᑎᑦᑎᐊᖓᑐᑦ ᓄᓇᒥ ᐊᖏᓂᖓᖃᓕᖅᓯᒪᒐᓗᐊᖅᑎᓪᓗᒍ, ᓄᓇᕗᑦ ᒥᑭᑦᑐᒥᒃ ᐃᓄᖕᓂᒃ ᐊᒥᓲᓂᖃᖅᐳᖅ (31,000 2009-ᒥ), ᐃᓚᖓᔪᑦ ᐃᓄᒋᐊᒃᓯᑎᑦᑎᓯᒪᖅᑯᐃᓴᓪᓗᓂ, ᐃᓚᔫᓈᓄᑦ. ᐃᖅᑲᓗᓐᓂ, ᑲᒪᓕᕆᓂᕐᒥ ᓯᕗᓕᖅᑎᐅᔪᑦ ᑕᑯᔭᐅᔪᓐᓇᖅᐸᒃᑎᓪᓗᒋᑦ ᐊᑐᓇᐊᒥ ᓂᐅᕕᕐᕕᖕᓂᓗ ᖃᐅᑕᒫᑎᒍᑦ, ᑲᒪᒃᑯᑦ ᐃᓚᐅᓂᖅᑎᑦᑎᑲᔪᒃᐳᑦ ᒥᑭᑦᑐᒥ ᓄᓇᓕᐅᔪᒥ ᑐᓐᖓᓇᖅᑑᓪᓗᑎᒃ, ᖃᓄᐃᓕᖓᓂᓇᔭᖓ ᑖᓐᓇ ᐃᓛᓐᓂᒃᑯᑦ ᑲᔪᓯᓂᖅᑎᐊᕈᓐᓇᖅᐸᒃᑐᖅ ᐊᑐᐃᓐᓇᓇᔭᐅᔪᓐᓇᕐᓗᓂ ᓄᓇᖅᑎᕐᑯᑎᖏᓐᓄᑦ!

ᐅᓪᓗᐃᑦ ᓯᕗᕐᖓᖏᓐᓂ

ᓄᓇ ᒫᓐᓇ ᓄᓇᓕᐸᐅᔭᐃᑦ ᐃᓂᒋᓕᖅᑕᖓ ᐊᑐᖅᑕᐅᓚᔪᓗᐊᓚᐅᓐᖏᓚᖅ ᐃᓅᖕᓂᑦ ᓄᓇᓕᓐᖑᓚᐅᖅᑎᓐᓇᒍ ᐱᔾᔪᑎᒋᓪᓗᒍ ᐊᕐᕌᒍᓖᓴᐅᔪᓄᑦ ᐃᓄᐃᑦ ᓂᕈᐊᕆᔭᖃᓚᐅᖅᓯᒪᖕᒪᑕ ᓄᓇᓕᕋᓛᖑᓗᑎᒃ, ᓯᐊᒻᒪᒃᑎᖅᓯᒪᐅᕈᓗᐃᔭᖅᑎᓪᓗᒋᑦ ᓄᓇᖅᑲᕕᖏᑦ ᐃᖅᑲᓗᐃᑦ ᐊᑲᓗᐊᓂ.

ᑕᐃᒪᐃᑐᐃᓐᓇᓇᐊᖅᑲᖅᓯᒪᑎᓪᓗᒍ ᕙᐃᑭᖕ ᓄᓇᓕᓃᓯᒪᑐᐃᓐᓇᓇᐊᖅᑲᖃᔭᕐᓂᖓᓕᖏᓐᓄᑦ, ᓯᕗᓪᓕᖅᐹᖅ ᓇᓗᓇᐃᖅᑕᐅᓯᒪᔪᖅ ᑕᓇᐅᑉ ᐊᑭᐊᓂᖕᓕᖅᓯᒪᔪᑦ ᑲᑎᖅᑲᑎᒋᔭᐅᓯᒪ-

arrière-poste lointain de l'administration coloniale. Elle est aujourd'hui devenue le centre du gouvernement de l'est de l'Arctique et a fait son entrée dans un nouveau monde, accueillant les dirigeants internationaux et composant avec l'impact de problématiques ayant vu le jour bien loin de là.

Bien qu'il forme un cinquième du territoire canadien, le Nunavut a une population réduite (31 000 en 2009), qui lui confère le caractère d'une grande famille élargie. À Iqaluit, où on peut croiser les dirigeants politiques sur la rue et dans les magasins tous les jours, le gouvernement revêt souvent le caractère amical d'une petite ville, situation qui peut parfois jouer en faveur des citoyens!

Les premiers jours

Les terres sur lesquelles la ville repose aujourd'hui étaient peu utilisées par les Inuits avant l'établissement d'une communauté permanente parce que, pendant des siècles, les gens préféraient vivre dans de petits camps répartis autour de la baie Frobisher.

Bien qu'il soit possible que les Vikings aient été présents dans la région, le premier contact confirmé avec les Européens remonte à l'époque où l'explorateur anglais Martin Frobisher a sondé la baie (qui porte aujourd'hui son nom), pendant trois étés consécutifs, de 1576 à 1578.

Although it is possible that the Vikings were in the area, the first confirmed contact with Europeans came when the English explorer Martin Frobisher probed the bay (which currently bears his name) for three summers between 1576 and 1578. Initially he was looking for the Northwest Passage but then changed his mind when he thought he had found gold-bearing ore. He returned home with his ships full of Baffin Island stone only to discover that he had made a major geological blunder and that the ore was worthless. Inuit certainly had no sympathy or respect for him. He kidnapped several of them, fought with others and left with an arrow in his buttocks as a souvenir from the local people who were amazed that a person would travel so far just to steal someone else's rocks!

From 1860 to 1862 an American, Charles Francis Hall, explored Frobisher Bay more fully, hearing the Inuit stories about Martin Frobisher and finding material evidence of his expeditions. By this time the native people were starting to become familiar with visits by foreigners. Whalers had already been present in the region for almost half a century, to be followed not long after by Christian missionaries and the RCMP. By 1914 the Hudson's Bay Company (which eventually set up stores throughout the Canadian

ᓂᑰᓂᖕᒋᓐᓄᑦ ᑯᐃᓐ ᓄᓇᖕᒐᓂᓐᖕᒎᖅᓯᒪᔪᖅ ᓇᒧᓐᖕᒐᕋᖅᑎ ᒫᑎᓐ ᕗᕈᐱᓱ ᖃᐅᔨᓴᖅᓯᒪᒍᖅ ᑲᖕᒋᖅᓱᖕᒐᓂᒃ (ᐊᑦᑎᖅᑕᐅᔾᔪ-ᑎᒋᓯᒪᓪᓗᓂᐅᒃ) ᐱᖕᒐᓱᑦ ᐊᐅᔪᓄᑦ 1576 ᐊᒻᒪᓗ 1578 ᐊᑯᓐᓂᖕᒋᓐᓂ. ᕿᓂᕋᓱᐊᓐᖕᒑᖅᓯᒪᒐᓗᐊᖅᑎᓪᓗᒍ ᓱᓪᓗᐊᓗᒃ ᐅᐊᓕᓂᕐᒥᑦ ᕿᑭᑦᑖᓗᒻᒧᑦ ᑕᓇᐅᒃᑯᑦ ᐊᖅᑯᑎᖕᒐᓂᒃ ᑭᓯᐊᓂ ᐃᓱᒪᒋᓯᒪᔪᓂ ᐊᓯᔾᔨᓚᐅᖅᓯᒪᔪᖕᒐ ᓇᓂᓯᓇᓱᒋᓐᓈᑎᓪᓗᒍ ᒎᓗᖅᖅᑐᒥᒃ ᓴᕕᕋᔪᒃᓴᒥᒃ. ᐊᖕᒋᕐᕋᒥᓄᑦ ᐅᑎᓕᓚᐅᖅᓯᒪᔪᖅ ᐅᒥᐊᕐᔪᐊᕐᑯᑎᖕᒋᓐᓂᒃ ᕿᑭᖅᑖᓗᒻᒥᓐᖕᒑᖅᓯᒪᔪᓂᒃ ᐅᔭᖅᑲᓂᒃ ᖃᐅᔨᓕᑕᐃᓐᓇᕐᓗᓂ ᐊᖕᒋᔪᒪᓇᒻᒥᒃ ᓄᓇᒥᓐᖕᒎᖅᓯᒪᔪᒥᒃ ᑕᒻᒪᖅᓯᒪᓂᖕᒐᓄᑦ ᐊᒻᒪᓗ ᓴᕕᕋᔪᒃᓴᔪᖅ ᐊᑭᑐᔪᒃᓴ-ᐅᖕᒋᑦᑐᕕᓂᐅᓪᓗᓂ. ᐃᓄᐃᑦ ᑖᔅᓱᒧᖕᒐ ᐃᒃᐱᒋᔪᓗᐊᓚᐅᖕᒋᑦᑐᑦ ᐃᖅᑲᒋᔪᖅᑲᓗᐊᕐᓇᑎᓪᓘᓐᓃᑦ. ᐊᒥᓱᓚᖕᓂᒃ ᑎᒌᒃᓯᒪᒐᖅ ᑖᒃᑯᓂ, ᐊᓯᖕᒋᓐᓂᓪᓗ ᐅᓇᑕᕐᑲᑎᕐᑲᖅᓯᒪᓪᓗᓂ ᐊᒻᒪᓗ ᐊᐅᓪᓚ-ᓕᓚᐅᖅᓯᒪᔪᕕᓂᖅ ᐅᐸᑎᖕᒋᑦᑎᒍᑦ ᐱᓯᒃᓯᒃᑕᕕᓂᐅᓪᓗᓂ ᑕᑯᐆᖅᑖᓇᓪᓗᓂᐅᒃ ᓄᓇᕐᖃᑎᐅᔪᓂᑦ ᐃᓄᐃᑦ ᑲᒪᔾᔪᑎᖃ-ᓚᐅᖅᓯᒪᖕᒪᑕ ᐃᓄᒃ ᐅᖕᒐᓱᒃᑐᒧᑦ ᐃᖕᒋᕐᕋᔪᕕᓂᖅ ᑎᓕᕆᐊᖅᑐᑐᐃᓐᓇᕐᓗᓂ ᐊᓯᖕᒐᑕ ᐅᔭᕐᑯᑎᖕᒋᓐᓂᒃ!

1860-ᒥᑦ 1862-ᒧᑦ ᒥᐊᓕᑲᕐᒥᐅᑕᖅ, ᓵᕈᔅ ᕗᕌᓐᓯᔅ ᕼᐋᓐ, ᐃᖅᑲᓗᖕᓂ ᐊᑕᖕᒋᐅᒪᓂᕐᓴᒃᑯᑦ ᖃᐅᔨᓴᖅᓯ-ᒪᓂᕐᓴᐅᒐᖅ, ᑐᓴᖅᓯᒪᓪᓗᒋᑦ ᐃᓄᐃᑦ ᐅᓂᒃᑳᖅᑐᐊᖕᒋᑦᑎᒍᑦ ᒫᑎ ᕗᕈᐱᓯᒥᒃ ᐊᒻᒪᓗ ᓇᓂᔭᐅᓯᒪᓂᖕᒋᓐᓄᑦ ᓇᓗᓇᐃᕈ-ᑎᒃᓴᒃᑲᓐᓂᐅᔪᑦ ᐃᖕᒋᕐᕋᓯᒪᓂᙱᖕᒋᓐᓄᑦ. ᑕᐃᔅᓱᒪᓂᐅᓕᖅᑎᓪᓗᒍ

Initialement, il était à la recherche du Passage du Nord-Ouest, mais il a changé d'idée lorsqu'il a cru avoir trouvé des minerais aurifères. Il est rentré avec ses vaisseaux pleins de pierres pour ensuite constater sa bourde géologique : les minerais n'étaient en réalité que des pierres sans valeur. Les Inuits n'éprouvaient ni sympathie, ni respect pour lui. Il en a enlevé plusieurs, s'est battu avec d'autres et a quitté les lieux une flèche à l'arrière-train, en guise de souvenir de la population locale, qui s'étonnait qu'on voyage si loin pour voler les pierres!

De 1860 à 1862 un Américain, Charles Francis Hall, a exploré la baie Frobisher plus rigoureusement, écouté les récits des Inuits à propos de Martin Frobisher et découvert des preuves de ses expéditions. À cette époque, les autochtones commençaient à être plus familiers avec les visites d'étrangers. Les chasseurs de baleine étaient déjà présents dans la région depuis près d'un demi-siècle et furent suivis peu après par les missionnaires chrétiens et la GRC. En 1914, la Compagnie de la Baie d'Hudson (qui allait par la suite établir des magasins dans l'ensemble de l'Arctique canadien) avait établi son premier poste de traite sur la baie Frobisher, jetant ainsi les assises de la dernière des trois institutions clés qui allaient transformer de façon irrévocable le mode de vie inuit traditionnel.

Arctic) had established its first trading post on Frobisher Bay, thus putting in place the last of the three key institutions which would initiate irrevocable change to the traditional Inuit way of life.

Cold War impact

By 1941 the population of Inuit camps around Frobisher Bay was 183 and the people, despite some contact with outsiders, were continuing to live a lifestyle totally dependent on the land. However, this was soon to change. In 1942 the United States Air Force began to build a large military airbase at Koojesse Inlet at the head of Frobisher Bay. It was supposedly to form part of the World War Two Crimson Staging route, a two-way project involving the transportation of warplanes to Europe and the ferrying of wounded back to the United States.

The Frobisher airbase was designed to house 800 servicemen and to handle 1,000 flights per month connecting North America and Europe. However, rapidly-improving aircraft technology and a change in flight route to the war zone via Goose Bay and Greenland meant that the brand-new, state-of-the-art Frobisher airfield could boast little more than a dozen flights a month, seemingly destined to become one huge white elephant.

In 1944 the airbase was sold by the USAF to the Canadian government.

ᓄᐊᖃᖅᑎᐸᒍᑦ ᓱᖏᑎᑎᖕᐊᓲᐸᓚᑕᐅᐳᖅᐱᐊᒍᑦ ᓄᐊᐸᑦ ᐊᑭᐊᓱᐊᓂᒃᑐᓄᑦ ᐳᓐᓕᐊᖅᑕᐅᖅᑕᖕᓄᑕᐱᓐᕈᓂᐤᓯ. ᐊᖏᓕᓴ ᐊᖏᑎ ᐊᖃᑐᓴᓚᓄᐊᑐ ᐱᑕᖅᖃᑐᖅᑎᖑᕈᒐᐅᑐᖅᒍ ᑕᒪᓕᓄᒃ ᕼᑲᓇᓕᓴ ᐊᕈᖃᑕ ᐊᓱᔮᔪᓯᓴᓕ, ᑭᒍᓯᓐᐊᖕᐊᒍᑕ ᓚᕼᖅᑕᐲᒐᓯᐳᖕ ᐊᕈᖅᔭᐱᐱᓇᓕ ᕙᓯᔮᐊᓂ. 1914-ᖕᒍᖕᑎᓂᒍ ᓂᐅᖃᖅᒍᒐᓕ (ᓂᐅᐊᖑᓇ ᕼᖅᐳᕙᖕᐊᑕᐄᑎᖕᐅᕐᐤᕼ ᑲᓇᑕᒃ ᐳᕐᐱᖅᑕᐳᑐᓇᑕᖑᓂᒐ) ᕼᖅᐳᑕᓕᖅᖃᖕᓕᑐᖕ ᕼᖏᔾᖅᕼᖅᑕ ᑕᐳᖃᕈᐊᐱᓇᓕ ᐊᕼᒍᐃᓇ, ᑭᒍᓴᖅᕙᔮᔾᓐᑕᐤᓯᒍ ᐊᕼᐸᑕ ᐊᑭᓂᖃᐃᐳᕐᓄ ᐁᑲᐤᐊ ᐋᐱᓴ ᐊᐳᕐᑐᖃᐳᔭᕐᓂᓇ ᐊᕐᕇᖕᕼᓄᓚᓯᑐᖅᒍᕐᓕᕐᓱ.

ᐅᓇᑖᕐᔭᐊᖕᒍᑕ ᐊᕼᑐᐱᕐᐳᕐᓕᓯᒍᓕ

1941-ᖕᒍᖕᑎᓂᒍ ᐃᓄᐃ ᐊᕼᒃᖏᓐᕼᑐ ᐃᓄᐃ ᓄᐊᖃᐃᓇᕐᕼᖕᐊᓇ ᐊᕼᒍᓴ ᕼᑐᕐᕼᓄ 183-ᖕᒍᐳᖅᒐᓕᓯᖕ ᐊᕐᓚᒍ ᐃᓄᐅ, ᕐᓕᑖᓇᖕᐱᖅᕐᓕᐱᒍ ᑲᓐᖃᔾᐊᓂᓚᓄᐊᖅᓐᓯᕐᕼ, ᐊᐱᐱᖅᔮᕼᖅᑎᖕᑕᐤᓯ ᐃᐳᕐᖃ-ᐊᓇᓕᐳᖅᐳ ᑐᓄᓕᕐᕼᖕᒐᐤᓯ ᓄᐊᕼᐤ. ᑖᐱᓚᖕᓄ-ᒐᖕᑎᓂᒍ, ᑕᓚᑕ ᐊᕐᕇᓇᐳᕐᓕᕐᓯᖅ. 1942-ᒐ ᕼᐊᓕᐳᕐᑕᓕ ᕼᖕᐳᑕᖅᓘᓯ ᐅᓇᑕᖅᔮᕼᖕᐊᑕ ᐊᕼᕐᕐᓕᑐᒐᒍᕐᕼ ᐅᓇᑕᖅᑐᕐᖏᑐᓯ ᕼᖕᐳᑕᖅᓘᕼᖃᓯᕼᓄᒃ ᓇᕐᕼᓯᑕᐊᖅᒍᕐᓯᖅ ᐳᕐᐱᑕᑐᓯ ᑭᖅᑕᔮᕼᓄ ᐃᐳᕐᖃᐅ ᐱᕐᖏᓇ. ᕼᖅᐱᖅᔮᑕᐤᓴᕐᖃᔾᐱᓇᖕ ᓄᐊᕐᖃᖕᒐᒐ ᐅᓇᑖᕐᔭᐊᖕᓄ ᓚᕐᕼᔮᕼᖕᓇ

Impact de
la guerre froide

Vers 1941, la population des camps inuits situés autour de la baie Frobisher était de 183 personnes et, malgré certains contacts avec les étrangers, cette population continua de mener un mode de vie entièrement fondé sur les ressources du territoire. Toutefois, les choses allaient bientôt changer. En 1942, les forces aériennes des États-Unis commencèrent à construire une importante base militaire à Koojesse Inlet, à la tête de la baie Frobisher. Cette base devait faire partie de la ligne d'étapes Crimson, au cours de la Deuxième Grande Guerre, projet prévoyant le transport des avions de guerre vers l'Europe et des blessés vers les États-Unis.

La base aérienne de Frobisher a été conçue pour héberger 800 préposés à l'entretien et traiter 1 000 vols par mois assurant la liaison entre l'Amérique du Nord et l'Europe. Toutefois, l'évolution rapide de la technologie aérospatiale et un changement de l'itinéraire des vols vers la zone de guerre via Goose Bay et le Groenland se traduisirent par une affluence d'à peine une dizaine de vols par mois, ce qui vouait la base à devenir un immense éléphant blanc.

En 1944, la USAF vendit la base aérienne au gouvernement canadien. Par

Nonetheless, seven years later, due to the growing Cold War with the then Soviet Union, the Americans returned to the Canadian Arctic and the Frobisher airfield finally came into its glory. Not only did it serve as a tanker base for refuelling B52 bombers in the air in case of an attack by Russia or its allies but it became the transportation and distribution centre for the construction of a North American radar defence network called the Distant Early Warning Line. At its peak the rejuvenated airbase was handling as many as 300 take-offs and landings per day.

At the same time, the Canadian government decided to build a village at Apex, five kilometres away, to provide housing, a nursing station, a school and other services for local people. However, after the Americans finally left in 1963, the government's focus shifted to the area near the airbase. Since the community of Frobisher Bay had been declared the

ᐊᖅᑯᑎᐅᓂᐊᕐᓗᓂ, ᒫᕐᕿᐃᓕᖅᑲᖓᔪᒥᒃ ᐱᓕᕆᐊᖑᓯᒪᔪᖅ ᐃᓚᐅᓂᖃᖅᑎᑦᑎᓪᓗᓂ ᐃᖏᕐᕋᔪᓕᕆᓂᕐᕕᐅᓂᖓᓄᑦ ᖃᖓᑕᓲᒃᑯᑦ ᐅᓇᑕᕿᑎᓂᒃ ᑕᓇᐅᑉ ᐊᑭᐊᓄᑦ ᐊᒻᒪᓗ ᐅᖅᑯᑎᐅᓪᓗᓂ ᐋᓂᖅᑐᑦ ᐅᑎᖅᑎᑕᐅᔫᓐᓇᖁᓪᓗᒋᑦ ᒥᐊᓕᒐᕐᓄᑦ.

ᐃᖃᓗᖕᓂ ᖃᖓᑕᓲᖃᕐᕕᒃ ᐋᖅᑭᒃᓱᖅᑕᐅᓯᒪᕗᖅ ᐃᓗᖃᖅᑎᑦᑎᓂᐊᕐᓗᓂ 800 ᐱᓯᑎᕋᖅᑎᓂᒃ ᐊᒻᒪᓗ ᑲᒪᔨᖃᕈᓐᓇᕐᓗᓂ 1,000 ᖃᖓᑕᓲᓂᒃ ᑕᖅᑭᑖᒧᑦ ᐊᑐᐊᖓᓕᖅᑎᑦᑎᓪᓗᓂ ᑲᓇᑕᐅᑉ/ᒥᐊᓕᒐᕐᒥᐅᑦ ᓄᓇᓕᕐᔭ-ᐊᖓᓂᒃ ᐊᒻᒪᓗ ᑕᓇᐅᑉ ᐊᑭᐊᓂᒃ. ᑕᐃᒪᐃᒃᑲᓗᐊᖅᑎᓪᓗᒍ, ᓲᒃᑲᔭᒥᒃ ᐱᐅᓯᑖᓪᓕᖅᐸᓪᓕᐊᑐᐃᓐᓇᖅᑎᓪᓗᒋᑦ ᖃᖓᑕᓲᓄᑦ ᓴᓇᔭᐅᓯᒪᓂᖏᑦ ᐊᒻᒪᓗ ᐊᓯᔾᔨᖅᑎᓪᓗᒍ ᖃᖓᑕᓲᓄᑦ ᐃᖏᕐᕋᕕᐅᖃᑦᑕᕐᓂᖓ ᐅᓇᑕᕖᔭᐊᖅᑐᓄᑦ ᐊᖅᑯᑎᖏᔭᐅᓪᓗᓂ ᒍᕐ ᐸᐃ ᐊᒻᒪᓗ ᑲᓵᓚᑦ ᓄᓈᑦ ᑐᑭᖃᓕᖅᓯᒪᕗᖅ ᓄᑖᖑᑦᑎᐊᕐᑐᖅ, ᓄᑖᖑᓂᖅᐹᖑᔭᑎᒍᑦ ᓴᓇᔭᐅᓯᒪᓂᖓ ᐃᖃᓗᐃᑦ ᖃᖓᑕᓲᖃᕕᖓᑦ ᑕᑯᖅᑯᔾᔨᓂᕐᓴᐅᔭᓐᓇᕐᓯ-ᒪᓚᓗᐊᖅᑎᓪᓗᒍ ᖁᓕᑦ ᒫᕐᖀᓪᓗ ᖃᖓᑕᓲᖃᖃᑦᑕᕐᓂᖓᓂᒃ ᑕᖅᑭᑖᑦ, ᐊᖏᓂᖅᐹᖑᓕᕋᔭᕐᓗᓂ ᓂᓇᐅᒋᔭᐅᓪᓗᓂ ᐊᑭᑐᔪᒻᒪᓇᐅᓪᓗᓂ ᑲᒪᒋᔭᐅᖃᑕᓇᐊᖃᕐᓂᖓᓄᑦ.

1944-ᒥ ᖃᖓᑕᓲᖃᕐᕕᒃ ᓂᐅᕿᑕᐅᓕᓚᐅᖅᓯᒪᕗᖅ ᒥᐊᓕᒐᕐᒥᐅᑦ ᐅᓇᑕᖅᑐᒃᓴᖏᓐᓂᑦ ᑲᓇᑕᐅᑉ ᒐᕙᒪᒃᑯᖏᓐᓄᑦ. ᑕᐃᒪᐃᒃᑲᓗᐊᖅᑎᓪᓗᒍ, ᐊᕕᓂᓖᑦ ᐊᑕᐅᓯᕐᓗ ᐊᕐᖁᒍᐃᑦ ᑭᖑᓂᐊᒍᑦ, ᐅᓇᑕᕖᔭᐊᕐᓂᖅᐸᓪᓕᐊᑎᓪᓗᒋᑦ ᓯᕕᐊᑦ ᔭᓂᐊᖕᖑᓚᐅᖅᓯᒪᔫᒐᓗᐊᒧᑦ ᕿᓯᐊᒥᐅᓂᒃ, ᒥᐊᓕᒐᕐᒥᐅᑦ ᑲᓇᑕᐅᑉ ᐅᑭᐅᖅᑕᖅᑐᖓᓄᑦ ᐅᑎᓕᓚᐅᖅᓯᒪᕗᑦ ᐊᒻᒪᓗ ᐃᖃᓗᖕᓂ ᖃᖓᑕᓲᖃᕐᕕᒃ ᐃᓕᓴᓇᔭᐅᔾᔭᕐᑎᐊᓕᓚᐅᖅᓯᒪᕗᖅ. ᐱᓯᑎᕋᑐᐃᓐᓇᕐᓇᓂ ᐅᖅᓵᕆᐅᖃᑦᑕᕐᓗᓂ ᐅᖅᓴᐃᒃᓇᖃᑦᑕᕐᓗᓂ B52 ᖄᖅᑎᑦᑎᓐᔭᑎᑦ ᖃᖓᑕᓲᓂᒃ ᓯᓚᒥ ᕿᓯᐊᒥᐅᓂᑦ ᑲᑐᔾᔨᖃᑎᒋᔭᖏᓐᓂᓪᓗᓐᓃᑦ ᐱᒋᐊᖅᑕᐅᑐᐊᕐᓂᖅᐸᑕ ᑭᓯᐊᓂ ᐃᖏᕐᕋᔪᓕᕆᓃᑉᐹᖑᓚᐅᖅᓯᒪᕗᖅ ᑐᓂᐅᖃᐃᑉᐱᐅᓕᖅᓯᒪᓪᓗᓂᓗ ᑲᓇᑕᒥ/ᒥᐊᓕᒐᐃᑦ ᓄᓇᓕᕐᔭᐊᖓᓂ ᓈᓚᐅᑎᖃᕕᖓᓂᒃ ᑕᐃᔭ-ᐅᓪᓗᑎᒃ ᐅᓇᑕᖅᑐᒃᓴᒃᑯᑦ ᓈᓚᐅᑎᖃᕕᖏᓐᓂᒃ. ᐱᒋᐊᖅᐸᓪᓕᐊ-ᓂᖃᓕᖅᑎᓪᓗᒋᑦ ᐱᒋᐊᓕᖅᑭᑎᒃᑲᓐᓂᕐᓯᒪᔭᖅ ᖃᖓᑕᓲᒃᑯᕕᒃ ᑲᒪᔨᖃᓕᒃᑲᓐᓂᓕᓚᐅᖅᓯᒪᒋᕗᖅ 300 ᐊᒥᓲᓂᖃᖅᑎᒋᔭᓂᒃ ᖃᖓᑦᑕᖃᑦᑕᖅᑐᓂᒃ ᒥᖃᑦᑕᖅᑐᓐᓂᓪᓗ ᐅᓪᓗᑖᑦ.

ailleurs, sept années plus tard, la Guerre froide avec l'Union soviétique s'intensifiant, les Américains retournèrent dans l'Arctique canadien et le terrain d'aviation de Frobisher allait connaître ses heures de gloire. Non seulement a-t-il servi de base de ravitaillement en carburant des bombardiers B42 en vol en prévision d'une attaque par la Russie ou ses alliés, mais devient en outre le centre de transport et de distribution du projet de construction d'un réseau de défense par radar du territoire nord-américain, appelé Réseau d'alerte avancé (DEW). Au sommet de sa gloire, la base aérienne traitait jusqu'à 300 décollages et atterrissages par jour.

Au même moment, le gouvernement canadien décidait de bâtir un village à Apex, à cinq kilomètres de là, pour offrir de l'hébergement, un poste de soins infirmiers, une école et d'autres services pour la population locale. Toutefois, après le départ des Américains, en 1963, le gouvernement s'intéressa davantage à la région située près de la base aérienne. Comme la communauté de Frobisher Bay avait été désignée comme bureau central des activités du gouvernement dans l'est de l'Arctique, les services furent graduellement retirés d'Apex dans une tentative infructueuse de fermer les installations qui s'y trouvaient.

headquarters of the government's Eastern Arctic operations, departments were slowly moved away from Apex in an unsuccessful attempt to close the settlement down.

Rapid growth

Frobisher Bay grew rapidly in the sixties. By 1971 it could boast two brand-new schools, a high-rise apartment complex and hotel and the fact that the Queen had come to initiate construction of the igloo-shaped Anglican cathedral. By 1987 the town's population had risen to over 3,000 and in that year its inhabitants decided to officially change the name of the community from Frobisher Bay to Iqaluit (meaning "Many fish"), thus reverting to the Inuktitut name that Inuit had always used anyway! In 1995 it was selected by territorial plebiscite to become the capital of the new territory of Nunavut. By 2009 its population had risen to over 6,000.

Centre of government

The Iqaluit of the twenty-first century is a veritable hub of activity by northern standards. As the territorial capital, and therefore officially a city, it houses the Nunavut Legislature, the headquarters of all government departments and the senior bureaucracy. It serves as the home for

ᑕᐃᒫᒃᓴᐃᓐᓇᐅᒻᒥᑎᓪᓗᒍ, ᑲᓇᑕᐅᑉ ᒐᕙᒪᒃᑯᖏᑦ ᓄᓇᓕᓐᖑᕐᑎᑦᑎᓇᓱᐊᓕᓚᐅᕐᓯᒪᔪᑦ ᓂᐊᖁᓐᖑᒥ, ᑕᓪᓚᒪᑦ ᑭᓛᒥᑕᓄᑦ ᐅᖓᓯᖕᓂᖅᑲᕐᑎᕆᔪᒥᒃ, ᐱᑕᖅᑲᕐᑎᑦᑎᓪᓗᑎᒃ ᐃᒡᓗᓂᒃ, ᐋᓐᓂᐊᕚᒥᒃ, ᐃᓕᓐᓂᐊᕐᕕᒻᒥᒃ ᐊᓯᖏᓐᓂᓪᓗ ᐱᔾᑎᖁᕝᕕᐅᔪᓂᒃ ᓄᓇᖅᑲᕐᑎᐅᔪᑦ ᐃᓄᖕᓄᑦ. ᑕᐃᒪᐃᒃᑲᓗ-ᐊᕐᑎᓪᓗᒍ, ᒥᐊᓕᒐᕐᒥᐅᑦ ᐊᐅᓪᓚᕐᑐᕕᓂᐅᑎᓪᓗᒋᑦ 1963-ᒥ. ᒐᕙᒪᒃᑯᑦ ᐃᒃᐱᕆᔭᖅᑲᓂᕐᓴᐅᓇᓱᐊᓕᓚᐅᕐᓯᒪᔪᑦ ᖃᖓᑕᓲᖅᑲᕐᕕᐅᑉ ᖃᓂᕆᔭᖕᒐᓅᖕᒑᓂᕐᓴᐅᔪᒧᑦ. ᑕᐃᒪᓐᖓᓂᑦ ᐃᖅᑲᓗᐃᑦ ᓄᓇᓕᖕᒐᑦ ᓇᓗᓇᐃᖅᑕᐅᒪᑦ ᐊᖓᔪᖅᑳᖅᑲᕐᕕᐅᓕᕐᓂᖕᒐᓄᑦ ᒐᕙᒪᒃᑯᑦ ᐅᑭᐅᖅᑕᖅᑑᑉ ᑲᓐᓇᖕᒐᓂ ᐊᐅᓚᓂᖓᔭᐅᔪᓂᒃ, ᐱᓕᕆᕝᕕᐅᔪᑦ ᓅᑉᐸᓪᓕᐊᕐᔮᓕᓚᐅᕐᓯᒪᔪᑦ ᓂᐊᖁᓐᖑᒧᑦ ᓄᓇᓕᐅᔪᖅ ᑲᔪᓯᓂᖅᑲᖕᒋᑦᑐᒃᑯᑦ ᒪᑐᔭᐅᓇᓱᑦᑎᐊᒻᒪᕆᒃᓯᒪᒐᓗᐊᕐᑎᓪᓗᒍ.

ᐱᕈᖅᐸᓪᓕᐊᒻᒪᕆᖕᓂᖕᒐ

ᐃᖅᑲᓗᐃᑦ ᐱᕈᖅᐸᓪᓕᐊᒻᒪᕆᓕᓚᐅᕐᓯᒪᔪᖅ 60-ᖏᓐᓂ. 1971-ᖑᓕᖅᑎᓪᓗᒍ ᒫᕿᓐᓂᒃ ᓄᑖᖕᓂᒃ ᐃᓕᓐᓂᐊᕐᕕᒃᑖᕐᓂ-ᖁᖅᓯᒪᓪᓗᓂ, ᐃᒡᓗᐊᓗᒻᒥᒃ ᐊᒻᒪᓗ ᑐᔪᕐᒥᕝᕕᒻᒥᒃ ᑯᐃᓐ ᑎᑭᓪᓗᓂ ᓴᓇᔭᐅᖁᓪᓗᒍ ᐃᒡᓗᕕᒐᐅᔭᕐᑎᑐᑦ ᐊᖓᓕᒃᑳᖑᑦ ᑐᒃᓯᐊᕐᕖᔪ-ᐊᖓᓂᒃ. 1987-ᖑᓕᖅᑎᓪᓗᒍ ᑕᐅᓐ ᐃᓄᐃᑦ ᐊᒥᓲᓂᖏᑦ ᖁᕚᓇᐊᖅᓯᒪᓕᓚᐅᕐᓯᒪᔪᖅ 3,000 ᐅᖓᑖᓄᑦ ᐊᒻᒪᓗ ᑕᐃᔅᓱᒪᓂ ᐊᕿᒍᖏᓐᓂ ᓄᓇᖅᑲᕐᑎᐅᔪᑦ ᐃᓕᓴᓇᔭᐅᓯᒪᔪᑎᒍᑦ

Croissance rapide

Frobisher Bay a connu une croissance rapide dans les années soixante. Vers 1971, elle pouvait s'enorgueillir de compter deux toutes nouvelles écoles, d'un complexe d'habitation de grande hauteur et d'un hôtel, ainsi que d'avoir accueilli la Reine, venue inaugurer le début des travaux de construction d'une cathédrale anglicane en forme d'igloo. En 1987, la population de la ville avait atteint 3 000 habitants, qui résolurent de changer officiellement le nom de la communauté de Frobisher Bay pour Iqaluit (qui signifie « endroit poissonneux »), revenant ainsi au nom de langue inuktitute que les Inuits avaient toujours utilisée de toute façon! En 1995, la ville était choisie par voie de plébiscite territorial pour devenir la capitale du nouveau territoire du Nunavut. En 2009, sa population était de 6 000 personnes.

Centre gouvernemental

La ville d'Iqaluit du vingt et unième siècle est une véritable plaque tournante, selon les normes nordiques. Comme capitale territoriale, et du fait même comme ville officielle, elle accueille la législature du Nunavut, le bureau central de tous les ministères, ainsi que le haut fonctionnariat. Plusieurs organismes inuits y ont leurs bureaux, elle relie les trois régions

many Inuit organisations, it links the three Nunavut regions of Qikiqtaaluk (Baffin), Kivalliq (west coast of Hudson Bay) and Kitikmeot (Central Arctic) and its influence extends throughout the Inuit circumpolar world.

As the transportation and communications centre of the territory (one that is only accessible by air most of the year), Iqaluit provides airlinks with all Nunavut communities, with Yellowknife and southern Canada, while its airport is world-renowned as a cold-weather testing centre for aircraft from all over the world.

But it is its status as the political centre of Nunavut that gives Iqaluit its real significance, stemming from the many years of political negotiations between Inuit and the federal government that culminated in the 1993 land claim settlement and the creation of Nunavut in 1999. Although the Government of Nunavut is

ᓄᓇᓕᐅᑉ ᐊᑎᖕᒋᓂᒃ ᐊᓯᔾᔩᓕᓚᐅᖅᓯᒪᔫᑦ ᕗᕈᐱᓯ ᐸᐃᒥᑦ ᐃᖃᓗᙵᓄᑦ (ᑐᑭᖃᖅᑐᖅ "ᐊᒥᓱᓂᒃ ᐃᖃᓗᓕᒃ"), ᑕᐃᒪᐃᒻᒪᑦ ᐊᓯᔾᔨᖅᑕᐅᓪᓗᓂ ᐃᓄᒃᑎᑐᑦ ᐊᑎᖕᒋᓄᑦ ᐃᓄᖕᓂᑦ ᐊᑐᐃᓐᓇᐅᔭᖅᑕᐅᖃᑦᑕᖅᓯᒪᔪᖅ! 1995-ᒥ ᓂᕆᐊᖅᑕᐅᓕᓚᐅᖅᓯᒪᔫᖅ ᐊᒡᕙᒃᑐᖅᓯᒪᓂᐊᓂ ᓂᕆᐊᒡᔪᐊᖅᑎᑦᑎᓪᓗᑎᒃ ᓄᑖᖅ ᐊᒡᕙᒃᑐᖅᓯᒪᓂᐅᓄᑦ ᐊᖕᒐᔪᖅᑳᖅᑲᖅᕕᐅᓕᕐᓂᐊᕐᓗᓂ ᓄᓇᕗᒻᒧᑦ. 2009-ᖑᓕᖅᑎᓪᓗᒍ ᐃᓄᐃᑦ ᐊᒥᓲᓂᖕᒋᑦ ᖁᕝᕙᓇᐊᖅᓯᒪᓂᖃᓕᖅᓯᒪᔫᖅ 6,000 ᐅᖓᑎᐊᓄᑦ.

ᒐᕙᒪᖃᕐᕕᐅᓂᖓᓄᑦ ᐱᓕᕆᕝᕕᒻᒪᕆᐅᓂᖓ

ᐃᖃᓗᐃᑦ, 21 Hᐊᓇᓚᐃᑦ ᐊᕐᕌᒍᓕᖅᑕᖕᒋᓐᓂ ᖃᓄᐃᓕᐅᕝᕙᓪᓗᐊᑕᐅᓕᖅᓯᒪᔪᖅ ᐅᑭᐅᖅᑕᖅᑐᒥ ᐱᔾᔪᓯᐅᔪᓄᑦ. ᐊᒡᕙᒃᑐᖅᓯᒪᓂᐊᓂ ᐊᖕᒐᔪᖅᑳᖅᑲᖅᕕᐅᑎᓪᓗᒍ ᐊᒻᒪᓗ ᑕᐃᒪᐃᒻᒪᑦ ᐃᓚᓴᕆᔭᐅᓯᒪᔪᑎᒍᑦ ᓄᓇᓕᐸᐅᔭᐅᓕᖅᓯᒪᓪᓗᓂ, ᐃᓂᖃᖅᕕᐅᔫᖅ ᒪᓕᒐᓕᐅᕐᕕᒻᒨᑦ, ᐊᖕᒐᔪᖅᑳᖅᑲᖅᕕᒃ ᒐᕙᒪᒃᑯᑦ ᐱᓕᕆᕝᕕᖑᑎᓚᖔᖕᒋᓐᓄᑦ ᐊᓯᖕᒋᓐᓄᓪᓗ ᐊᖕᒐᔪᖅᑲᐅᑎᓂᕐᓴᐅᔪᑦ ᒐᕙᒪᓕᕆᔨᐅᔪᓂᑦ. ᐱᔨᑦᑎᕋᖅᐸᒃᐳᖅ ᐊᖕᒋᕐᕆᕆᔭᐅᓪᓗᓂ ᐊᒥᓱᑦ ᐃᓄᐃᑦ ᑲᑐᔾᔨᖃᑎᒋᖕᒋᓐᓄᑦ, ᐊᒃᑐᐊᖕᒍᓂᖃᖅᑎᑦᑎᓪᓗᓂ ᐱᖕᒐᓱᑦ ᓄᓇᕗᒥ ᐊᒡᕙᒃᑐᖅᓯᒪᓂᐊᓃᑦᑐᓄᑦ ᕿᑭᖅᑖᓗᒃ, ᑭᕙᓪᓕᖅ (Hᐊᑦᓴᓐ ᐸᐃ ᐱᖕᖑᓐᓇᖅᐸᓯᖕᒍᓂ) ᐊᒻᒪᓗ ᕿᑎᕐᒥᐅᑦ (ᐅᑭᐅᖅᑕᖅᑑᑉ ᕿᑎᖅᐸᓯᐊᓃᑦᑐᑦ) ᐊᒻᒪᓗ ᐊᐅᓚᔾᔭᐃᔭᐅᓯᒪᓂᖕᒍ ᐅᖓᕙᓇᐊᖅᓯᒪᔪᖅ ᐃᓄᐃᑦ ᓯᓚᕐᔪᐊᒥ ᐅᑭᐅᖅᑕᖅᑐᖕᒋᓐᓂ.

ᐃᖕᒋᕐᕋᔪᓕᓐᓂᕕᐅᑦᑕᖅᑎᓪᓗᒍ ᐊᒻᒪᓗ ᑐᓴᐅᒪᖃᑦᑕᐅᑎᓕᓐᓂᕕᐅᑎᓪᓗᒍ ᐊᒡᕙᒃᑐᖅᓯᒪᓂᐊᓄᑦ (ᑖᓐᓇ ᓯᓚᐃᓐᓇᒃᑯᑐᐊᖅ ᐊᖅᑰᓴᕕᐅᔪᓐᓇᖅᐸᒃᑐᑐᐊᖅ ᐊᕐᕌᒍᓕᒫᐸᓗᒻᒥ). ᐃᖃᓗᐃᑦ ᖃᖓᑕᔫᖅᑕᐅᔪᓐᓇᖃᑦᑕᕐᔪᖅ ᑕᒪᕐᒥᓕᒫᖅ ᓄᓇᕗᑦ ᓄᓇᓕᖕᒋᓐᓂᑦ, ᐃᓚᒌᔭᐅᓪᓗᑎᒃ ᔭᓗᓇᐃᕝ ᐊᒻᒪᓗ ᑲᓇᑕᐅᑉ ᓂᒋᐊᓂᑦᑐᑦ, ᖃᖓᑕᔫᒃᑯᕕᖕᒐᑦ ᓄᓇᕐᔪᐊᕐᒥᐅᓂᑦ ᖃᐅᔨᒪᔭᐅᓪᓗᓂ ᐃᒃᑮᓐᓇᖅᑎᓪᓗᒍ ᓯᓚᒧᑦ ᖃᐅᔨᓴᕐᕕᐅᔪᓐᓇᖃᑦᑕᕐᓗᓂ ᖃᖓᑕᔫᓄᑦ ᓄᓇᕐᔪᐊᓕᒫᒥ.

du Nunavut que sont Qikiqtaaluk (Baffin), Kivalliq (côte ouest de la Baie d'Hudson) et Kitikmeot (centre de l'Arctique) et son influence s'étend au-delà du monde inuit circumpolaire.

En sa qualité de centre des services de transport et de communications du territoire (accessible uniquement par voie aérienne pendant la plus grande partie de l'année), Iqaluit offre des liaisons aériennes avec toutes les communautés du Nunavut, avec Yellowknife et le sud du Canada. De plus, son aéroport est un centre d'essais par conditions de froid nordique pour la plupart des avions du monde.

C'est principalement son statut de centre politique du Nunavut qui confère à Iqaluit son importance. Ce statut est le fruit de plusieurs années de négociations politiques entre les Inuits et le gouvernement fédéral qui ont été couronnées par la ratification de l'Accord sur les revendications territoriales, en 1933, et par la création du Nunavut, en 1999. Bien que le gouvernement du Nunavut soit officiellement un gouvernement public, il offre en réalité aux Inuits l'autonomie gouvernementale, puisque les Inuits constituent 85 % de la population. Ce gouvernement est unique à plusieurs égards, ce dont font foi l'accent mis sur l'utilisation de la langue inuktitute, la politique *Inuit Qaujimajatuqangit* (qui intègre l'expérience traditionnelle au

officially a public institution, in reality it offers self-government to Inuit since they constitute 85% of the population. It is unique in several ways, reflected in its emphasis on use of the Inuktitut language, in its policy of *Inuit Qaujimajatuqangit* (which incorporates traditional experience in modern decision-making), in its decentralisation of government departments to smaller communities and in its preference for operating by consensus rather than through political parties in the Legislative Assembly. The Government of Nunavut now works closely with the governments of the Yukon and Northwest Territories, with the three often presenting a joint political stance in dealings with Ottawa.

Modern community

As a modern community, Iqaluit can offer a well-equipped hospital, emergency services, a number of hotels and restaurants, several schools and daycares, the Arctic College, a museum, a visitors' centre, a library, arenas, a curling rink, a movie theatre, art galleries, cable and satellite T.V., high speed Internet, cell phones, service clubs, a variety of stores, a host of recreational and entertainment options and probably more computers for a place its size than anywhere in Canada!

At the same time, many Inuit customs are still very much a visible part of

ᑭᓯᐊᓂ ᖃᐅᐃᓕᓴᓕᒃᑯᓐ ᒐᕙᒪᖃᖅᑎᑕᐅ-ᑐᓛᐊᑦᖃᖅᖢᓂᒃ ᓄᓇᖅ ᐃᖃᓗᖕᓂᒃ ᐱᒻᒪᕆᐅᑎᑦᑎᓇᓱᒃᖢᖅ. ᐱᑕᖃᑦᑎᑦᑎᖦᒍᒋᐊᖅᖢᓄ ᐊᒡᒍᖅ ᐊᖅᖢᒐᓄᒃ ᒐᕙᒪᓄᕐᒥ ᐋᖅᑭᒃᑕᐅᒪᒐᖕᒃᒃ ᑖᖃᓇᐅᖕᒃ ᐃᓄᖏᓇᒃ ᒐᕙᒡᑦᑭᑦᖃᔪᖓ ᑖᓇ ᐃᓴᒃᑎᑕᐅᒪᒃᖢᓄ 1993-ᒥ ᓄᓇᑦᓯᐊᓇᖏᓄᒃ ᐊᖕᖃᒃᑎᑦᔪᓂᒃ ᐊᒻᒪᖅ ᓄᓇᖏᑦ ᐱᖕᖢᑎᑕᐅᒃᖢᓄ 1999-ᒥ. ᓄᓇᖏᑦ ᒐᕙᒪᖏᒃ ᐃᓯᒃᓯᖅᐳᕐᒃᖃᓄᒃ ᒃᑊᑲᑦᔮᓄᒃ ᒐᕙᒡᑐᖃᔪᖕᒋᓄ, ᐱᒃᓕᐋᑯᓄᒃ ᑐᖕᖅᑮᒃᔪᖅᐳᕐᕗ ᖃᒻᒃᓯᒃ ᒐᕙᒃᖃᖕᖢᒃᑮᓄᕐᒥᒃ ᐃᓇᖕ 85 ᐳᕐᒃᖢᒃ ᐊᒻᒃᖃᓄ-ᖦᐅᔪᕐᒃᖢᒃ ᐃᓄᖕᒃ. ᐊᒃᖃᐅᕐᖅᒃᖃᖕᖃᖅᕕ ᐊᒻᒃᑲᓇᐃᒃ ᐱᔅᒃᔪᐅᔪᓄᒃ, ᑖᒃᖃᐃᓄᖃᖕᖃᖕᖢᓄᖕ ᐱᒻᒪᕆᐅᒃᓄᖕᖃᒃᕿᓇᕐᒃ ᐃᓄᐃᒃ ᐅᖅᑮᔪᖅᖢᒃ ᐊᔪᖅᑕᐅᔪᖕᖃᖕᖅᑮᒋᖕᖢᒃ, ᐊᔪᐃᓇ ᐃᓄᐃᒃ ᖃᑊᐃᓕᔪᔮᖕᕿᓄ (ᖃᖕᖅᖢᑎᕿᖢᓄ ᐃᓄᒃᑯᔪᖕᖅᑯᒃᑯᒃ ᖃᑊᖅᕿᑕᐅᕿᖃᓄᒃ ᑖᓄᐃᑕᒃᔮᖕᔪᒃ ᐃᓯᒃᓗᖃᐃᓄᖕᒃᒃᒃ), ᒐᕙᒃᒃᔪᒃ ᐱᒃᓕᐋᓂᕐᒃ ᓴᕿᒃᖢᖕᖃᑕᐅᕿᓄᖦᖢᕐᒃ ᒥᒃᖃᕐᒃᐅᐃᒃᒃ ᓄᓇᐅᑏᒃᓄᒃ ᐊᒻᒃᖅ ᓂᐊᓄᖕᕿᕐᖢᒃ ᐊᐳᒃᑎᓄᕐᒃᒃ ᐊᖕᖅᒃᖃᒃᒃᔪᐊᓇᖕᔪᒃᑯᒃ ᐊᔪᖕᖅᕿᕐᒃᔪᖕᒃ ᒐᕙᒃᒃᔪᒃ ᑭᔪᖅᖅᒃᒃᖕᕿᕐᒃᒃ ᒪᓄᐃᒃᑕᐅᔪᖕᒃ. ᓄᓇᖅ ᒐᕙᒃᓂᒃ ᒪᓇ ᐱᒃᓕᒃᖃᖕᖃᖅᕗᖅ ᔮᖕ ᓄᖦᔮᖕᖢᒃ ᒐᕙᒃᒃᔪᖕᖅᕿᕐᒃ, ᐊᖕᖢᕐᒃᓄᒃ ᓄᒃᖃᖕᖃᒃᖕᓄᖕᕿᕐᖢᖢᒃ ᑭᒃᔮᔪᖕᖅᖃᒃ ᒐᕙᒃᒃᔪᖕᒃ ᐱᒃᓕᒃᖃᖅᕿᖢᖕᖢᒃ ᐊᖕᖅᒃᖃᖕᖢᒃᖅᔪᖕᖅᐅᕿᔪᖕᖅᒃᒃ ᐊᒃᔪᕿᒥ.

processus décisionnel moderne), la décentralisation des instances gouvernementales dans les petites communautés et sa préférence pour le fonctionnement consensuel plutôt que par l'interaction de partis politiques à l'Assemblée législative. Le gouvernement du Nunavut collabore maintenant étroitement avec les gouvernements du Yukon et des Territoires du Nord-Ouest, ces trois entités faisant souvent des représentations solidaires dans leurs échanges avec Ottawa.

Communauté moderne

Communauté moderne, Iqaluit peut offrir un hôpital bien équipé, des services d'urgence, un bon nombre d'hôtels et de restaurants, plusieurs écoles et garderies, le Collège de l'Arctique, un musée, un bureau touristique, une bibliothèque, des arénas, une piste de curling, une salle de cinéma, des galeries d'art, la télévision par câble et par satellite, Internet haute vitesse, la téléphonie cellulaire, des clubs de service, divers magasins, un éventail d'activités récréatives et de divertissement, ainsi que, probablement, plus d'ordinateurs, pour une ville de cette taille, qu'à tout autre endroit au Canada!

Par ailleurs, plusieurs coutumes inuites demeurent très visibles dans la vie de la communauté. La chasse, la pêche et le piégeage se poursuivent toute l'année durant, on y porte encore des vêtements

community life. Hunting, fishing and trapping continue year round, skin clothing is still worn and women continue to carry their young in traditional *amoutiit*. Carvers can often be seen working outside their homes, native arts and crafts can be bought in most stores and galleries, while festivals and displays of Inuit dance, song, drama and fashion are regular events.

Blending of cultures

The community has managed to pioneer a blending of Inuit and *Qallunaat* ways so that much of its unique flavour lies in its cross-cultural contrasts and combinations. This is a place where Inuktitut, French and English can be heard in daily use; where men in caribou-skin parkas go hunting wild animals while jet aircraft fly overhead; where sealskins are scraped and cleaned in homes that may also house a television and a computer.

ᐅᓪᒪᐅᑕᖅᑐᒥ ᓄᓇᓕᒃ

ᐅᓪᒪᐅᑕᖅᑐᒥ ᓄᓇᐅᕗᑦ, ᐃᖅᑰᐃᑦ ᑐᖕᖑᑎᒃᑕᖅᑲᕐᒐᖅᓴ ᐱᖖᒋᒃᑎᑦᑕᖅᑕᒐᒥᑉ ᐊᖅᓄᐊᕙᔪᒡᒥᑉ, ᑐᐊᒥᐊᖅᑐᓕᓂᒪᓐᔾ ᐱᐱᑦᑎᖅᑎᑎᑉ, ᑐᔾᕐᒐᐅᕝᑕᓂᑉ ᓂᓚᖅᑐᑑᖅᓂᓐᔾ, ᐊᒐᓪᒪᓕᓴᑦ ᐃᓗᓂᐊᖅᓯᑦ ᐸᐃᓂᓈᑉ, ᐅᑉᐅᑦᑎᖅᑐᒥ ᕐᐃᑦᑐᖅᖃᕝᓴᑉ, ᑕᑯᕝᒪᖅᕝᓴᑉ, ᐳᒦᐊᖅᖃᐳᒡᖆ ᖅᐅᖅᖃᐳᒡᓴᑉ, ᖅᒥᖅᕐᐊᐱᖅᖃᕝᓴᑉ, ᐊᖅᒦᖃᑕᒥᔾᑦ, ᑐᐊᖅᓴᑉ, ᑕᓂᒃᕝᓴᑉ, ᓴᐊᖖᔪᐊᒐᒥᑉ ᓂᕿᐊᖅᓂᑦ, ᐅᐊᖅᔪᖅᑐᑎᔾ ᖖᒡᓚᖖᑐᓐ-ᑕᐅᒥᖅᖆᑐᒥᔾᑐ ᑕᑲᖖᓂᖕᑦᑉ, ᖑᑉᕐᖅᑎᒥᒋᔾ ᖅᖁᖅᑕᖓᒡᑐ ᐱᑐᕐᒪᕐᕈᓴᓂᒐᒥᑉ, ᑐᖅᖃᐱᕝᑕᓐᖅᖅᐅᐊᑐᖅᕝᑐᑐ ᐱᖖᒡᔪᐊᓂᓇᖕᒡ ᐱᐊᖖᒡᔪᐊᕝᐊᒐᒡᔾ ᓂᐳᐊᐱᖅᐅᕙᑉ ᐊᖅᒪ ᖅᖃᕝᐅᑐᖅᖃᐅᑕᖅᖆᕝᐅᕝᐊᑉ ᓄᓇᐅᑉ ᐊᖅᒐᓯᓗᔾᒥᑐᖅᔾ ᐊᓕᒦᐃᐊᓂᑉ ᑲᒪᑌᒥ!

ᑕᐊᓕᒪᐃᕐᑎᓐᔾᔾ, ᐊᒐᕝᑦ ᐃᓄᐊᑉ ᓯᕐᒥᖖᕐᒋᑉ ᐳᑕ ᑕᑯᖕᑐᐅᖖᑐᖖ ᐃᓕᖅᓴᑐᖖᓯᓂᑉ ᓄᓇᐃᑉ ᐃᒥᓯᖖᑐᓐ. ᐊᖅᖁᖖᑐᖖ, ᐃᖅᒡᑐᓯᖖᑐᖖ ᒦᖖᐊᖖᑐ-ᐊᖅᖃᑉᖖ ᑲᕝᓯᓂᖅᖃᑉᑉ ᐊᖅᖅᓴᒡᖆ, ᒦᖅᕝᑐᓂᑉ ᐊᖖᕕᑉ ᓯᕐ ᐊᑐᖅᑕᐅᖖᑉ ᐊᖖᒡ ᐊᕐᐃᑉ ᓄᑕᖅᕝᒦᓂᑉ ᐊᒦᖖᖅᖆᕝᑉ ᐊᒐᒦᐅᖅᑐᖖᖅᑎᒐᒡᑦ. ᓴᐊᖖᒡᔪᐊᖅᑐᒥ ᑕᑯᖖᒡᐊᖅᖃᖖᑕᓐᑉ ᐊᖖᕐᖖᕐᑉ ᓯᕐᑕᖖ, ᓄᐊᖅᖖᐅᐊᒐᖅᖖ ᓴᖖᒡᑐᖖᖅᕝᑉ ᓴᖖᐅᖖᑐᖖᒡᔪᐊᖖᖅᕝᐅᒐᖖᕝᑐᖖ ᓂᖕᑕᖅᖆᑕᖖ ᑕᐊᕝᐅᒐᒃᑉ ᓂᐅᑉᖖᐅ ᑕᑯᖖᒡᔾᓴᖖᓂᒐ, ᐊᖅᑐᐊᖖᕐᓂᑉ ᐊᖖᒡ ᑕᑯᖖᒡᓂᖅᑕᐅᖅᑉ ᐃᓄᑉ ᒡᒥᑕᒦᖖᑉ, ᐱᕐᒦᖖᑉ, ᐃᒡᑐᐊᐊᖖᑐᖖ ᐱᖖᒡᔪᐊᖅᑉᑉ ᐊᖅᖆ ᐊᖖᒡᓯᖅᐊᖖᕝ ᖅᖃᓐᐅᑕᖅᖅᓂᒡᐳᐃᖅᖅᖆᑎᖖᔪᒐᖖᑉ.

ᐱᖖᒡᕝᔾᓂᖖᒡᕝᕝᐊᓂᑉ ᑲᑎᖖᖁᓚᕐᖖᑦᑎᓂᖅ

ᓄᓇᒦᑉ ᑲᑎᖖᕐᖕᖅᑎᑉᑎᕝᕝᖖᖆᔾᒥᒡᔾᐊᖅᖆ ᐃᓄᐃᑉ ᖅᒡᓴᒐᖖ ᐱᐊᐳᖅᖕᕝᐊᓂᑉ ᐊᖅᔾᐊᖅᑐᖖᒦᓚᖅᓐᖕᐅᔾᑉ ᑐᖕᒦᓗᖅᑉᓂᖖ ᐱᖖᒡᕐᑕᖖᐱᐊᓂᖖᖅᒐᖅᖖᑐᑉ ᐊᖅᖕᕝᖖᕝᖖᐊᓐᒐᖅᖖᓂᖖᖆᖖ ᑲᑎᖖᓴᖖ-

en peaux d'animaux et les femmes continuent de porter leurs enfants dans un *amoutiit* traditionnel. Les sculpteurs peuvent souvent être vus à l'œuvre à l'extérieur de leur maison, on peut acheter des œuvres d'artisanat autochtone dans la plupart des magasins et galeries, alors que les festivals et spectacles de danse, chant, théâtre et mode inuits sont régulièrement à l'affiche.

Bouillon de cultures

La communauté a veillé à mettre en place un mélange de modes de vie inuits et de *Qallunaat*, de sorte qu'une grande partie de sa saveur unique tient aux contrastes et combinaisons interculturels. On peut y entendre les langues inuktitute, française et anglaise quotidiennement; des hommes en parkas de peau de caribou y vont chasser du gibier, alors que des jets les survolent; des peaux de phoques sont grattées et nettoyées dans des maisons où on pourra également trouver un téléviseur et un ordinateur.

C'est probablement l'accès à ce mélange inhabituel de trois cultures, jumelé à un sentiment prédominant de liberté et d'espace, qui incite les gens à s'y établir en nombre sans cesse croissant. On peut en avoir un avant-goût à Toonik Tyme, ce festival annuel tenu chaque année en avril pour célébrer la fin de l'hiver. Cet événement offre une excel-

It is perhaps the access to this unusual blend of three cultures, coupled with an over-riding feeling of freedom and spaciousness, that draws people to make their homes here in ever-increasing numbers. A taste of this can be gleaned at Toonik Tyme, the annual festival held each April to celebrate the end of winter. The occasion provides an excellent opportunity to capture aspects of both the traditional and modern Arctic, with the chance to see dogteam and snowmobile races, igloo-building competitions and a host of other activities. In many ways Iqaluit offers the best of both worlds. It lends easy access to the rugged northern landscape, its people and their traditions, while at the same time providing the conveniences and modern facilities of a Canadian territorial capital.

Nature dominates

However, despite man's best efforts to make a mark on the North, it is still the over-whelming power and beauty of the land which dominates everything North of Sixty and it is well worth joining up with friends or hiring a local outfitter to get a taste of it by dogteam, snowmobile or boat.

Parks, historical sites and the northern flora and fauna are all within relatively easy access most of the year. In spite of the rapid growth of the community, a short walk can quickly take one

ᓚᖅᑎᑕᕆᓚᖕᖓᒦᕐᓂᓗᑦ. ᑖᓐᓇ ᐃᓂᐅᑉᓯᖅ ᐃᓄᖕᑎᑦ, ᐅᐃᕕᑎᑦ ᖃᓪᓗᓈᑎᕐᓗ ᐅᖅᑲᐅᓯᕐᒃᑕᕈᖕᒃ ᑐᖕᓴᐅᕐᑕᖕᑕᕈᖕᓂᓗ ᖅᑲᑦᒪᑕᓗᒃ; ᐊᓗᑎᑦ ᔪᒐᔪᑕᖅᕐᓚᖕᓈ ᐊᓄᔭᓇᕐᑕᕈᖕᑐᔾ ᓄᕐᑲᖅᕐᑐᑎᑦ ᐅᐱᕐᓂ ᐳᕐᓇᖕ ᖃᖕᓚᕐᑕ ᓗᔾᑎᑦᑎᖕᓗᔾ; ᖅᐱᓚᖕᓂᑦ ᑕᖕᖢᕐᒃᑕᑐᒐ ᖅᖅᐅᑦᕐᑕᐅᑐᖕᒻᒥ.

ᐃᒻᒦᑎᑦ ᐊᑐᐊᖕᖑᕐᕈᖕᒋᕐ ᑖᕐᓯᑐᖕᓈᑎ ᐊᖅᖡᑦᑐᕐᑐᓚᔾ ᑲᓂᖕᓇᓚᖕᕐᔩᐊᓚᕈᖕᑦᑕ ᐱᓂᕐᑎᓯ ᐱᖕᒃᑐᕐᓚᕐᑕᕐᓈᑕᖕᔩᐊᕐᑕᕐᓂ, ᐃᓚᒐᐱᕐᓈᒐᓗ ᐊᔾᓯᒪᖅᖡᖅᓄᖕᓂᖕᒻᕐ ᐃᓄᕐᐱᖕᖅᓯᑎᐊᖕᓇᖅᕈᖕᓕᓗ, ᐃᓄᖕᓈᑎᑦ ᐊᓚᕐᕐᖅᓇᖕᑕᕈᖕᕐᒐᕐᑐᕐᑕᖕᒃᑐᖕᖅ ᑕᒻᒥᓐ ᐊᒻᕈᖅᕈᐸᖕᐦᑎᐅᐊᖕᑦᒐ. ᑕᒻᒣᖕᔪ ᖅᑲᕐᐅᖕᐦᑕᕐᑐᕐᕐᓈᑦᖕᔭᖕ ᑐᓄᖕᑦ ᑕᐃᒻᒥ, ᐊᕐᔪᑑᑕᑎᑦ ᓚᖕᑕᕐᐅᓈᒐᐅᕐᑲᕐᕈᑕᕐᓈᑎᑦ ᐅᐸᑕᑎᑦ ᓚᖕᑕᕐᐅᓈᒐᐅᕐᑲᕈᕈᖕᒻ ᐅᖅᐅᑦ ᐃᖕᓚᖕᕐᒃᓗᖕᖅ. ᓚᖕᑕᕐᐅᓈᒐᐅᕐᑲᕐᖕᑎᕐᖕᓈᑎᑦ ᐱᑕᖅᕐᖕᑦᑎᑦᑕᕐᖕᖕᑕᕐᖕᖢᓈ ᓚᐹᕐᓚᖕᑦᑕ ᑕᕐᖕᕐᖕᑎᑦᕐᖕ ᐊᑕᖕ ᐃᓚᖕᓗᑐᖕᖕᑕᖕᑎᑦ ᐅᕐᓚᖕᑕᕐᖕᖕᒥ ᐅᖕᖕᒃᑐᖕ, ᑕᕐᖕᑕᕐᖕᒐᕐᖕᑎᖕᖕᑦ ᖅᐱᔾᓚᔾᑦ ᖅᒐᑦᑕᕐᖕᑕᔾᖕᓈ ᓚᕐᖕᓈᖕᐱᖕᑕᖕᑎᖕᑦ, ᐃᔾᓗᑦᒪᖕᔾᖕᑕᖕᑎᖕ ᐊᖕᓗᓚ ᐊᕈᖕᔪᐊᒃᖕᑕᖕᑦᑕ ᖅᑕᐃᐅᑦᓈᕈᖕᖕᑐᖕᖕ. ᐊᒣᕐ ᐱᐅᕈᐅᖕᑕᐅᑦ ᐃᖕᓚᖕᑎᑦ ᑐᖕᖕᔾᑐᖕᖕᑕᕐᖕᑐᕐᖕᒥ ᐱᐅᖕᖕᖕᖕ ᐊᖕᓗᖕ ᓄᓈᖕᑕᐊᖕᐅᔾᖕᑕᖕᖕᑦ. ᐊᑐᐊᖕᖑᕐᕈᖕᖕᖕᑎᖕᑦᑎᖕᖕ ᐅᕐᔮᖕᑕᔾᖕᑦ ᐅᖅᐅᖕᖕᑦᖕᒃᑐᖕᖕᒥ ᓄᓚᐅᕐᑦᑕᖕᑎᑦ, ᐃᖕᖕᒻᕐᓈᓈᑦ ᐊᖕᓗ ᐃᓚᖕᖕᖢᕐᕈᖕᔾᖕᖕᓈᑎᖕᑦ, ᑕᒻᒥᓚᖕᕐᒥᕐᖕᓚᑦᔾ ᓚᖕᑕᕐᖕᑎᑦᖕᑎᑦᖕ ᐊᑐᐊᖕᖑᕐᑕᐅᕐᖕᑕᖕᑐᖕ ᐅᖅᐅᕐᕈᕐᐅᖕᑕᕐᖕᖕᒥ ᐱᑕᓚᐊᖕᑕᕐ ᕐᑲᐃᑐᖕᖕᖢᓚᖕᓚ ᐊᖕᖕᓚᕐᑕᖕᖅᕐᖕᕐᖕᖕᓈᑐ.

ᓄᓈᐅᑦ ᓯᖕᒐᓂᕐᑲᐅᓈᖕᑦᑲ

ᑕᒻᒥᐃᖕᖅᓗᐊᖅᕐᑎᖕᓗ, ᐃᖕᖕᑦᒃ ᐱᓇᔾᐊᖕᕐᑎᖕᖅᕐᒃᓗᖕᖢᓂᖕᑐᕐ ᐅᖅᐅᖅᕐᑕᔾᖕᖅ ᓚᔾᓚᓈᖕᖅᑲᐅᑕᔾᒐᔾᒐ, ᓯᕐ ᓄᓈᐅᑦ ᐱᐅᔾᓇᖕᖅᕐᖕᓚᖕᖡᖕᓂᖕᖅᒃᓗᖕ ᐱᖢᖕᖕᓚ ᓯᖕᒐᓂᕐᖅᖕᕐᓂᕐᑦᓈᖕᕐᖅ ᕐᐱᑦᑕᓈᖕ ᓚᕐᑐᖕᑦ ᐅᖅᐅᖅᕐᑕᔾᖕᖅ 60-ᖕᖢᐦᑐᒐ ᐊᖢᔾᖢ ᐊᖕᑐᕐᖕᑐᑦᑎ ᐊᖕᖅᕐᕐᑕᖕᔾᕐᖕᕐ ᑲᖕᑲᓂᕐᓗᕐᑦ ᓯᖕᖕᖢᖕᑐᐅᖕᑦ ᐅᕐᕈᖕᖕᖕᑦ ᐃᖕᖕᒃᑲᓇᐃᕐᖕᑲᖕᐦᑎᑕᖕ ᓄᓈᖕᒃᖕᖕᑐᖕᔾ ᐊᔾᐅᓚᖕᑎᖕᑕᕐᕈᖕᑦᕈᖕ ᑕᐃᔾᕐᕐᐅᔾᐊᖕᕐᑎᑦᖕᖅᐅᖕ ᖅᑐᖕᖕᖅᖕᔾᖕᑦᖕᑦ, ᖅᐳᑦᑕᖕᔾᖕᖕᑐᖕ ᐅᕐᖕᕐᖕᑐᔾᖕᖕᖅᕐ.

lente occasion de prendre le pouls de l'Arctique traditionnel et moderne, la possibilité d'assister à des courses d'attelages de chiens, de construction d'igloos, et de participer à une foule d'autres activités. De diverses façons, Iqaluit, offre le meilleur des deux mondes. Elle constitue une porte d'accès aux régions austères du Nord, à leur population et à leurs traditions, tout en offrant la commodité et les installations modernes d'une capitale territoriale.

La nature domine

Toutefois, malgré les efforts soutenus de l'homme pour laisser sa marque dans le Nord, la puissance et la beauté du territoire dominent tout au nord du 60e parallèle, et il vaut la peine de se joindre à des amis ou d'engager un pourvoyeur local pour le découvrir en attelage de traîneau, en motoneige ou en bateau.

onto the tundra and into the quiet, timeless world of the Arctic, where animals and birds still abound. From June through September, the rolling hills around the city are ablaze with the colours of plants and flowers, providing a miracle of beauty after being buried for so long under ice and snow.

The new North

But Nunavut is no longer protected by the cold from outside influences. It is affected on a daily basis by decisions and events occurring in other parts of the world, by issues such as industrial air pollution, anti-sealing legislation and the search for bio-fuels. Global warming has already made an impact on the Arctic and its peoples. The Inuit way of life is linked to a cold climate so rising temperatures affect both their homeland and their identity simultaneously. Changing ice and

ᒥᕐᖑᐃᖅᓯᕐᕖᑦ, ᐃᑦᑕᕐᓂᓴᖃᕐᕕᐅᔪᓪᓗ ᐊᒻᒪᓗ ᐅᑭᐅᖅᑕᖅᑑᑉ ᐱᕈᖅᓯᐊᖏᑦ ᐆᒪᔪᖏᓪᓗ ᑕᒪᕐᒥᓕᒫᖅ ᑐᓐᖓᓂᖃᖅᐳᖅ ᐃᑳᕐᕕᐅᔪᓐᓇᕐᑐᒃᑯᑦ ᐊᕐᕌᒍᓕᒫᐸᓗᒻᒥ. ᓄᓇᓕᒃ ᓱᒃᑲᔪᑎᒍᑦ ᐱᕈᖅᐸᓪᓕᐊᓂᖃᒻᒪᕆᒃᑲᓗᐊᖅᑎᓪᓗᒍ, ᓇᐃᑦᑐᒧᑦ ᐱᓱᕝᕕᒃᓴᖅ ᓄᓇᐃᓐᓇᕐᒧᐊᕈᑎᐅᔪᓐᓇᖅᐳᖅ ᐊᒻᒪᓗ ᓂᐱᖃᖏᑦᑐᒧᐊᕐᓗᓂ, ᐃᑲᕐᖃᖏᑦᑐᖅ ᓄᓇᕐᔪᐊᖓᓄᑦ ᐅᑭᐅᖅᑕᖅᑐᒥ, ᓂᕐᔪᑎᖃᐅᑦᑎᐊᕐᓗᓂ ᑎᖕᒥᐊᖃᐅᑦᑎᐊᓇᓪᓗᓂ. ᔫᓂᒥᑦ ᓯᑎᐱᓇᒧᑦ, ᖃᖅᑲᓪᓚᐃᓪᓗ ᓄᓇᓕᐸᐅᔭᒥ ᑕᑯᒃᓴᐅᓂᖃᑦᑎᐊᓕᖅᑎᑦᑎᕚᒃᐳᑦ ᑕᖅᓴᖃᑦᑎᐊᕐᑐᓂᒃ ᐱᕈᖅᑐᓂᒃ ᐱᕈᖅᓯᐊᓂᓪᓗ, ᐱᑕᖃᖅᑎᑦᑎᓪᓗᓂ ᑲᒪᓇᖅᑐᒥᒃ ᐱᐅᔪᐊᓘᓂᖓᓂᒃ ᐊᑯᓂᒻᒪᓇᐅᔪᒧᑦ ᓴᐅᔭᐅᓯᒪᓚᐅᕈᓗᐊᖅᑎᓪᓗᒋᑦ ᓯᑯᑉ ᐊᐳᑎᐅᓪᓗ ᐊᑖᓂ.

ᓄᑖᖅ ᐅᑭᐅᖅᑕᖅᑐᖅ

ᑭᓯᐊᓂ ᓄᓇᕗᑦ ᓴᐳᒻᒥᔭᐅᓯᒪᔪᓐᓃᕐᒪᑦ ᐃᒃᐹᓇᖅᑐᒧᑦ ᓯᓚᑎᖕᖓᓂᙶᖅᓯᒪᔪᓂᑦ ᐊᐅᓚᔾᔭᐃᔭᐅᓯᒪᓂᓇᔭᖕᖓᓄᑦ. ᐊᒃᑐᐃᔭᐅᓯᒪᕗᖅ ᖃᐅᑕᒫᖅᓯᐅᑎᓄᑦ ᐃᓱᒪᓕᐅᕆᔭᐅᓂᒃᑯᑦ ᖃᓄᐃᓕᐅᕐᓂᕆᔭᐅᕙᒃᑐᓄᑦ ᐊᓯᖕᒥᓐᓂ ᓄᓇᕐᔪᐊᒦᑦᑐᓂᑦ, ᐱᔾᔪᑎᒃᓴᐅᔪᑎᒍᑦ ᓱᕐᓗ ᓴᓇᕝᕕᐊᓗᐃᑦ ᐳᔪᕐᓗᓕᐅᖅᑐᑦ, ᓇᑦᑎᖏᓯᐊᕐᓂᕐᒧᑦ ᓄᖅᑲᖅᑎᑦᑎᓇᓯᐊᕐᓂᒃᑯᑦ ᒪᓕᒐᓕᐊᕆᔭᐅᔪᑎᒍᑦ ᐊᒻᒪᓗ ᐳᓪᓕᓕᕐᓄᑦ ᐅᖅᓯᐊᓗᒃᓯᐅᕐᓂᕐᒥᑦ. ᓄᓇᕐᔪᐊᑉ ᐅᖅᑰᓯᐸᓪᓕᐊᓂᖓ ᐊᒃᑐᐃᓂᖃᖅᑎᑦᑎᓯᒪᓕᓚᐅᖅᐳᖅ ᐅᑭᐅᖅᑕᖅᑐᒧᑦ ᐃᓄᖁᑎᖏᓐᓄᑦ. ᐃᓄᐃᑦ ᐃᓅᓯᕆᔭᖓᑦ ᐊᒃᑐᐊᖓᓂᖃᕐᒪᑦ ᐃᒃᑮᓇᕐᑐᖅ ᓯᓚᖓᓄᑦ ᐊᒻᒪᓗ ᐅᖅᑰᓯᐸᓪᓕᐊᓂᖓ ᐊᒃᑐᐃᓂᖃᖅᐳᖅ ᓄᓇᒥᔭᖓᓄᑦ ᐃᓕᓴᕆᔭᐅᔪᑎᖏᓐᓄᓪᓗ ᑭᖑᓕᓐᓃᒃᓯᖅᑐᒥᒃ. ᐊᓯᔾᔨᖅᐸᓪᓕᐊᓂᖓ ᓯᑯᑉ ᐊᐳᑎᐅᓪᓗ ᖃᓄᐃᓕᖓᓂᖏᓐᓂᒃ ᐃᖏᕐᕋᓯᐊᕐᓂᒃᑯᑦ ᐊᑦᑕᓇᖅᓯᔾᔪᑕᐅᐸᓪᓕᐊᑐᐃᓐᓇᖅᐳᖅ, ᓄᓇᐅᑉ ᐊᓯᐅᐸᓪᓕᐊᓂᖓ ᐅᓗᕆᐊᓇᖅᓯᔾᔪᑕᐅᓪᓗᓂ ᐃᓪᓗᖁᑎᓄᑦ, ᐊᑐᕆᐊᓄᑦ ᒥᑦᑕᕐᕕᖕᓄᓪᓗ, ᐃᓚᖏᑦ ᐆᒪᔪᖁᑎᑐᖃᕆᔭᐅᔪᑦ ᐃᓱᒪᒋᔭᐅᓯᒪᓕᕐᒪᑕ ᐊᑦᑕᓇᖅᑐᒦᑦᑐᐃᓐᓇᕆᐊᖃᓕᕐᓂᖏᓐᓄᑦ ᐊᓂᕐᓂᖃᕐᓇᖅᑑᑉ ᖁᑎᓐᓂᖓᑕ ᓄᖑᐸᓪᓕᐊᓂᖓᓄᑦ ᑐᓐᓂᖅᑯᑎᖅᓯᒪᓕᕐᓗᓂ ᐃᓄᐃᑦ ᓯᕿᓂᐅᑉ ᖃᐅᒪᓂᕐᒪᓂᖕᖏᑦᑐᒥᑦ ᓴᖅᑭᔮᕐᓂᖅᓴᐅᐸᓪᓕᐊᑐᐃᓐᓇᕐᓂᕐᓄᑦ. ᓯᑯᑉ ᐊᐅᒃᐸᓪᓕᐊᓂᖓ ᓯᓪᓗᐊᓗᒃ ᐅᐊᓕᓂᕐᒥᑦ

Les parcs les sites historiques, ainsi que la faune et la flore locales sont tous à une portée relativement accessible, presque toute l'année. Malgré la croissance rapide de la communauté, une courte marche peut rapidement vous mener dans la toundra et dans l'univers paisible, intemporel de l'Arctique, où les animaux et les oiseaux foisonnent aujourd'hui encore. De juin à septembre, les terrains ondulés qui entourent la ville miroitent des couleurs de la végétation et des fleurs, qui offrent à la vue un prodige de beauté, elles qui ont été ensevelies si longtemps sous la glace et la neige.

Le nouveau Nord

Mais le froid ne protège plus le Nunavut des influences extérieures. Il est affecté quotidiennement par des décisions et événements survenant dans d'autres parties du monde, par des problèmes tels que la pollution de l'air, les lois contre la chasse aux phoques et la recherche de biocombustibles. Le réchauffement de la planète a déjà eu un impact sur l'Arctique et sur sa population. Le mode de vie inuit est adapté à un climat froid. Le territoire ainsi que l'identité des Inuits sont aujourd'hui affectés par le réchauffement du climat. Les changements affectant la configuration des surfaces de glace et de neige rendent les déplacements plus périlleux,

snow patterns now make travel more dangerous, land erosion threatens buildings, roads and airstrips, some traditional animal species are thought to be at risk while ozone layer depletion contributes to increasing human UV exposure. Ice melt in the Northwest Passage may possibly open the North to some international shipping, which not only creates sovereignty and military implications for the area but throws an uncertain light on the future of Inuit who have lived in the region for centuries.

One rapidly emerging face of change in Nunavut is the growth of mineral exploration on land and the search for resources such as diamonds, gold, uranium and iron ore. As the Arctic ice melts, the fingers of this exploration start to reach under water too, searching for the enormous reserves of oil and gas known to lie there. Under the 1993 land claim, Inuit have the guaranteed right to negotiate jobs, benefits and royalties in any mineral exploration on Inuit lands. However, mineral development is a two-edged sword which will require balancing the benefits of royalties and well-paid mine-related jobs with the impact such development may have on the Inuit way of life and their homeland.

Survival for many Inuit in today's world not only still involves the quest for food in a harsh environment but also

ᖀᑉᖃᑕᔪᖕᒍᑦ ᑕᓇᑉᑲᔭᑦ ᐊᒡᔭᑎᖕᒐ ᒪᑐᖅᔆᕐᐊᑎᑐᑕᐊᓇᐊᖃᑉᑲᓛᔪᓄ ᐅᑭᐅᖅᑕᑐᒡᒥᑉ ᒦᕐᔭᖕᒥᒃ ᓄᐊᔆᖕᐊᒥ ᐅᒐᔪᖅᐊᑐᑦᖃᑎᓄᐅᑎᐅᔪᒥᑉ, ᖅᖃᐳᒍᐊᖃᖅᔭᖕᒃᒐᒥᑐᒑᑦ ᐊᐊᓇᔆᖕᖃᖅᑦᑕᖅᒐᖓᓄᑎ ᐊᓕᔭᔆᓯ, ᑐᐅᒑᖅᔭᒐᔆ ᐊᔆᐊᐅᖅᖃᔆᖓᓇᓇᐅᑐᑎᖕᒃᔭᕐᒃᒐ ᐊᐅᐊᑦ ᖕᖃᑉᑐᑯᑎᐅᖃᓇᖕᔆᓱᓇᑦᖃᖓᔆ ᐊᑐᖅᐃᔪᑦᐊᑐᖕᒐ ᓄᐊᖅᔆᔪᕐᔭᑦ ᐊᖕᖃᒍᔪᖕᔭᖅᐊᔭᑦ.

ᔭᖅᐊᔭᒃᒥᑉ ᖅᖃᑉᑦᐊᔆᐊᖅᖃᓂᔆᖕᓇᒐᖕᔭᖅᑐ ᓄᐊᔪᑦ ᐊᔆᑉᖕᐊᖃᓇᓂᔆᖕᓇᒐ ᓕᖃᔆᖃᑐᑐᐊᖕᒐᔆᒐᑦ ᐅᔪᖕᒃᔭᑦᐅᔆᖕᒃ ᓄᐊᒥᑉ ᐊᒻᓗ ᖀᖅᔆᖓᔆᖕᒐ ᓄᐊᒥᑐᑕᑦᑕᖕᒥᑉ ᔆᓄ ᐅᔪᖃᑦ ᐳᑎᖅᔆᓇᖃᑦᐊᔪᑦ, ᔆᒍᐊᑦ, ᐊᓂᔪᔭᐊᑐᖅᒥᑉ ᐊᒻᓗ ᔆᐊᖅᔭᑉᔆᔆᐊᑦ. ᐅᑭᐅᖅᑕᑭᓂᔆᐅᑕᔪᔆᖅᔆᐊᔆᑕᖕᒃᑦᐊᑐᑦ, ᑕᒪᓇ ᖀᓇᑉᔆᐅᐅᔆᖕ ᑎᖅᑕᐊᑎᕐᔆᔭᓱᔆ ᐃᐅᑎᐅᑦ ᐊᖃᖃᑕᖅᑐᖅ, ᖀᓇᔆᖃᐃᑎᐊᓱᑐ ᐊᔆᔭᐊᔭᖃᓂᔆᒥᑉ ᐅᖅᔆᐊᔪᑉᖃᔭᐅᐅᔆᖕ ᖅᑕᐅᓕᔭᐅᑎᔆᒍ ᐊᑎᔆᖅᖃᓇᖓᑦ. 1993 ᓄᐊᔆᖕᒍᑦ ᐊᖕᖃᖅᒥᑎᖅᐅᑎᖅᔭᐅᖃᐅᐊᔆᔭᓯᒥᒡ, ᐃᐅᑦ ᐊᔆᓇᑎᔆᐊᓇᓂᔆᔆᔭᖅᑐ ᐊᖅᖀᖅᔆᖃᖃᓱᑎᖕ ᐊᖃᐅᐊᑭᔆᖓᓄ, ᐊᐳᔆᐊᑐ ᓇᓂᔆᖃᖃᑎᐅᖃᐅᑎ ᐊᓇᓇᖕᔆᓱᖃᔆᔪ ᐅᔪᖅᔆᐊᑎᖅᖃᐊᖅᐊᑎᐊ ᐃᐅᑦ ᓄᐊᒍᑦᑎᒥᒪᔆ. ᑕᒪᓇ ᐅᔪᖅᒃᔭᐅᓂᔆᖅ ᐊᔆᔪᖕᔆ ᐳᐊᖃᑉᔆᖅ ᓇᓗᑐᑎᑕᐅᔆᐅᐊᖅᔆᓄ ᐊᐳᔆᔭᑦ ᓇᔆᖅᖃᐊᑎᐊ ᐊᒻᓗ ᐊᖀᓇᖅᔆᖃᑐᐊᔆᑦ ᐅᔪᖅᔆᐊᔆᓄ ᐊᓇᓇᖕᔆᒐᐊᑐ ᐊᔆᐅᔪᖅᔆᖕᔆᖕᔆᓂ ᔆᓄ ᐅᔆᔆᐊᔆᓇᖃ ᑕᒪᓇᐃᐅᑎᐊᓇᓂᔆᖕᔆᒍ ᐃᐅᑦ ᐃᐳᓇᔪᖕᔆᒥᔆ ᓄᐊᔆᖕᒍᔆ.

in having to face the unpredictability of constant change in almost every aspect of life. As the territorial capital and major transportation centre, Iqaluit is the funnel for much of this change that comes to Nunavut. It is where the bridging often takes place between outside influences and northern traditions, sometimes meeting with success, sometimes with mixed results, but in the process giving the community a unique eclectic character.

A place to visit

Nunavut has much to contribute to the rest of Canada that is refreshingly different but it is still often described as one of the country's last hidden gems, easily missed despite its size. The power of the land, its links with Inuit culture and its subtle, sometimes stark, but ever-changing beauty make Nunavut at times seem

ᐃᓅᓯᐊᕐᓱᓂᖅ ᐊᒡᒐᖏᑦ ᐃᓄᖕᒧᑦ ᐅᔾᒥᒑᖅᑐᒥ ᓄᓇᓕᕐᔪᐊᒃᒥ ᐃᓚᐅᓂᖃᖅᑎᑎᐅᖁᐊᖕᖏᖕᒃ ᓂᒃᐸᓴᐅᑦᖤᐊᖕᓂᒃ ᐱᓂᓪᖃᒥ ᐊᖃᑎᒃᔭᖕᖏᓂ ᑭᕐᐊᔅᑕᐅᖅ ᓴᐱᖅᑕᖃᖅᒍᓪᓴᓂᖅ ᐊᓚᐅᑦᓚᒃᖅᔭᐊᖕᖏᒃᖃᓂᐊᖅᑐᒃ ᑕᒪᒡᒥᐃᔅᒃᔪᖕ ᐃᓅᓂᖠᖕᖓᓂᒃ. ᐊᐃᑎᓪᒥᓚᐊᐃᖅ ᐊᖕᓛᖃᖃᖓᖠ ᐊᒥᓗ ᐊᖕᖏᓂᖅᒃᔭᖕᖤᒥ ᐃᖕᖠᖅᔭᑎᖃᒃᐋᐁᓪᓂᐊᒍᒃ, ᐃᖃᐃᑦ ᑐᖃᑧᐁᐅᖕᖅ ᑕᓚᒃᒃᖠ ᐊᖕᓯᖃᒃᓚᐊᐆᐅᔭᐃᒃ ᓄᐊᓪᑲᒃᐸᖅᖤᐅᖤᒃᔪᖕᐃ. ᐊᒃᒥᒍᖅᖃᖓᖕᖠᒍ ᕇᐊ ᑕᐃᑲᐃᐃᖕᐃᖅᒃᖠᓗᒍ ᕇᐁᐅᓄ ᖤᖕᕇᖓᐂᖠᖕᖤᖃᒃ ᐊᐃᐊᖠᐃᖤᓂᖕᖠᒃ ᐊᒥᓗ ᖃᐆᖃᖅᑆᒃᒍ ᐃᖕᖅᖤᖃᖤᒃᐸᐅᔭᐃᖅ, ᐃᖃᖕᖅ ᒃᖠᕇᖕᖃᓂᐊᖤᖃᖃᖤᓂᖕᖃ, ᐃᖃᖕᖅᖠ ᓂᒍᕇᒃᖤᐊᐃᒃ ᖃᒃᐃᖤᓪᕇᖕᖤᖃᖕᐸᐄᖃᓂᖠᖠᐃᓇᖕᖤᒍ, ᕇᐁᐅ ᖤᖃᖓ ᐆᐊᓕᖠᖠ ᐊᐆᖃᐃᖤᖠᓂᖅᖃᖠᖃᖅᒍᐃᐅ ᐆᔭᐅᖕᐅᖕᖠᕇᑉᐅᐊᖅᒃᔪᖕᖃ ᐃᐄᖤᖃᖃᓪᑎᐄᖤᖃᖤᖠᒍᐃ.

ᓄᓇ
ᖤᒥᖃᐁᖃᐃᖃᐃᖕᖅ

ᓄᓇᖅ ᐃᑲᔪᖃᖕᖤᓚᒃᔭᑕᐄᓚᐄᖃ ᑲᓂᖤᐊᐄ ᐁᖃᖕᓂᒃᐅᖤᓂ ᖤᖃᖤᖤᒃᔭᖅᒍᖤᐄᖤᖤᒍᖤᖃᒃ ᕇᐁᐁ ᓈᓄᐄᖃᖅᖃᐅᖤᖤᖃᐃᒃᐃᖅᒍᐃᖕᖤ ᖤᐃᖅ ᓄᓇᖅᖤᐊᖤᓂᖕᖤ ᓇᓂᖃᒃᐁᖃᖕᖅᒃᔪᖠᖤᐅᖕᖠ ᖃᖤᖕᖃᖤᖃᐊᖤᖕᖠᖠᖤ, ᓇᖃᖅᐁᐅᖃᖕᖃᐅᖕᖃᖕᖤᖠᖃᖤ ᐊᖤᐃᖕᓇᖕᖤᖠᐃᖤ. ᓄᓇᖅ ᕇᐊᖤᖃᖕᖤᖠ, ᐊᖕᖅᐁᖃᖤᓂᖕᖤᖃᖤᖤᖅ ᐃᐄᖃ ᕇᖤᖤᐊᐆᖕᖅ ᐊᒥᓗ ᐊᖃᖅᖃᖕᖅᒍᐃᖕᖃ, ᐃᖃᖕᖅᖤᐄᖤᒍ ᕇᐊᖃᑲᑎᖕᐄᖃᖃᖕᐅᖃᖕᖅᒍᐄᖕᖤ, ᕇᐁᐆᖃ ᐊᐃᖤᓂᖕᖤᐄᖤᖤᖤᐅᐁᐁᖕᖤᖕᖠ ᐄᐅᐁᐆᓂᖕᖤᖠ ᓄᓇᖤᒍᐃ ᐃᐄᖃᖕᐅᖃᐅᐄ ᑕᖤᖕᖤᐄᐅᖃᖃᖤᐅᐃᐅᖤᖃᖕᐁᖕᐅᐃᐃᖃᖕᖅ ᐊᖕᕇᖠᖤᒍᐅᖤ ᓄᓇᖤᖤᐊᖤᐊᖕᖤᖕᖤ. ᐃᖤᖕᖤᖤᐁᖃ ᐄᖃᐄᖃᖕᖤᒃᕇᐄᐁᖤ ᕇᐊᖤᖃᐅᖤᒃᖃᖕᖤ ᓄᓇ - *No Strange Land* - ᐃᖤᖕᖤᖤᖤᐅᖃᕇᖤᖠᖠᐆᖕ ᖕᐆᐃᖕ ᑕᖤᖤᖤᒍ ᐃᖤᖕᖤᖤᖃᐆᐆᖤᒃᖕᖤᖠᕇᐁᒍᐄᖠᖃ ᐁᑲᖠᐅᐄ ᐊᖕᖃᒍᐄ ᐅᖤᖠᐃᑎᐄᓂᖕ ᐃᖃᖤᐁᐁᖤᖤᐄᖤᐊᖕᖅ ᐁᐁᖕᖤᖕᑐᒃᕇᖤᖤᐊᖕᖠᐄᖤ ᐅᖤᖠᖕᐄᖤᖤᐄᖕᖤᐄᖃ ᓂᐄᖤᐄᖤᐅᖤᖃᖤᖃᐄᖃᖕᖤ ᕇᐄᖤᖕᖤᐄᖃᐄᖤᒃᖤ, ᖤᐄᖤᐄᖕ ᐊᖤᐅᖤᖤᖤᖃᖤ ᐃᐄᖤᐄᖕᖤᐃᒍ,

et l'impact de ce développement sur le mode de vie des Inuits sur leur territoire.

La survie de nombreux Inuits dans le monde d'aujourd'hui dépend encore de la recherche de nourriture dans un environnement hostile, mais aussi du caractère imprévisible des changements constants qui affectent presque tous les aspects de la vie. Comme capitale territoriale et important centre des services de transport, Iqaluit fait œuvre d'entonnoir où survient ce vent de changement qui souffle sur le Nunavut. C'est souvent là que se trouve le point de convergence des influences extérieures et des traditions nordiques, parfois avec bonheur et succès, parfois en produisant des résultats mitigés, mais donnant à la communauté un caractère éclectique du fait même.

Un endroit à visiter

Le Nunavut peut enrichir le reste du Canada d'un apport important et rafraîchissant, mais il est encore souvent décrit comme une des derniers joyaux cachés du pays, facilement oublié malgré sa taille. La puissance de ce territoire, ses liens avec la culture inuite ainsi qu'avec une nature subtile, parfois austère, mais toujours changeante, lui confèrent le caractère d'un autre univers. Quelques lignes que l'on doit à l'œuvre « *No Strange Land* » de Francis Thompson, écrite il y a plus d'un siècle, nous rappellent comme il

other-worldly. Lines from '*No Strange Land*' by Francis Thompson written over a century ago remind one of how easy it is sometimes to overlook unexpected treasure, a fact not lost on Inuit who, having lived so often on the edge of survival, have learned the importance of carefully observing what Nature has to offer.

The angels keep their ancient places
Turn but a stone and start a wing
'Tis ye, 'tis your estranged faces
That miss the many-splendoured thing.

The territory of Nunavut was created to give Inuit back control of their homeland and to provide them with the hope of a secure future within Canada. If Nunavut is all about hope, then Iqaluit, as the seat of government, is surely the key to that hope for northerners. For others, who have been intrigued by the mystery of the Arctic, Iqaluit now provides a convenient gateway to it. As the territorial capital, with its modern facilities set amid Inuit traditions, today's Iqaluit offers a taste of both old and new for everyone in Canada's Eastern Arctic.

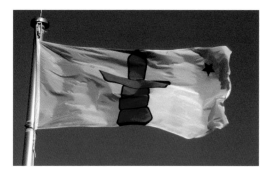

ᐃᓄᐃᓯᐊᖃᑦᑖᖅᓯᒪᓕᕐᓗᑎᒃ, ᐃᓕᑦᑎᒥᓕᐳᑦ ᐱᒻᒪᕆᐅᓂᖓᒥᒃ ᖃᐅᔨᓴᑦᑎᐊᕆᔪᒪᓂᖅᓯᒥᒃ ᓄᓇ ᑭᓯᒥᒃ ᑐᓂᖅᑯᑎᖃᕐᓇᒪᖔᕆᒥᒃ.

ᐊᐃᕝᕆᓪ ᐱᕝᒥᑎᖏᑦ ᐃᓄᑦᔮᖕᓘᒡᓖᕝᒥᒃ
ᓴᖅᑯᓯᓂ ᐅᔭᕋᓐᔪᐃᓯᐅᖅᓯᖅ ᐊᒻᒪᓗ
ᐃᑭᖅᑖᖅᓯᕝᕙᓪᕙᑦᓯᖅ
ᐃᖕᐊᑦ, ᐊᔪᐴᓯᖅᓯᓪᕚᕝᒥ ᑭᐊᕝᔭ
ᑕᑯᕝᓇᔾᓯᕆᔭᕝᑐᑉ ᐊᒡᕝᒃ ᐱᐅᔭᒻᓕᓐᐊᒡᕝᒥᒃ ᑭᓯᐅᕚᓂᒃ.

ᓄᓇᕝᑦ ᐱᕝᕆᕝᒍᖅᑎᑕᐅᕝᖅᓯᓕᕝᕇᖅ ᐃᓄᐃᑦ ᑐᖅᑎᖅᑎᑎᐊᕝᒎᐊᒡᓂᐅᖅ ᐊᐅᐸᕝᑎᖅᓯᕝᓯᕆᖏᒥᒃ ᓄᓇᕝᓯᓕᓄᒃ ᐊᒻᒪᓗ ᓂᓇᐳᓂᖅᖃᓐᑎᐅᕝᖃᓐᐊᖏᕝᓘᖏ ᓯᕝᐅᕝᖃᕝᓂᐊᕝᓯᖅᓐᒍ ᑲᓇᑕᑉ ᐃᓗᐊᓂ. ᓄᓇᕝᑦ ᐱᕝᓯᑎᖕᐳᕝᕙᑉ ᓂᓇᐳᓂᖅᒥᒃ, ᐃᑉᕇᐳᑕᐳᑎᓪᓘᒎ ᒪᖃᑦᖃᐃᐳᕝᒋᖅ, ᒪᓪᐴᕝᕝᖅᑎᐳᕝᒢᐊᖏᕝᐊᕝᐳᖅᕝ ᓂᓇᐳᓂᐳᐳᐃᕝᓯᓂ ᐅᑭᐳᖅᑯᓯᕝᒋᕝᓯᒪᓪᒎ, ᑐᖅᔭᓯᒢᐃᐳᕝᓯᕝᕝᖅᒥ ᐅᑭᐳᖅᓯᖅᒎᕝ ᓇᓄᐊᓯᕝᓘᓂᒎ, ᐃᖅᒎᐃᑦ ᒪᖄᐳᖅᑐᒥ ᐱᑎᖅᑎᑎᑐᕝ ᐊᑐᐊᖃᓕᕝᓯᖅᒎᒃ ᐊᕝᔪᑐᐸᓐᓓᖅᒎᑦ ᓯᕝᓄᒎᒃ. ᐊᕝᓯᕝᖃᕝᓓᒎᐊᓂ ᐊᕝᓕᔭᖅᕃᕝᓯᐊᐳᓐᑎᓪᒎᒎ, ᐳᓪᒎᒢᐃᕝᐸᕝᖅᑐᕝ ᐱᑎᓂᑭᖅᒥᕝᓐᒎᒎ ᐃᓄᐃᑦ ᐃᓐᑎᖅᑯᖅᕝᕃᕝᒋᖅᑕ ᐊᑕᓄᕝᓘᒎᑦ, ᐅᑐᓖᕝᐳᕝᒢᓂᒎ ᐃᖅᒎᐃᑦ ᑐᖅᓂᒎᖃ-ᑎᕝᓯᕝᒋᖅᑕᐳᕝᕝᓯᖅ ᖃᐳᖅᕃᖅᑎᕝᕝᒋᖅᐃᕝᕝᒋ ᐊᕝᒎ ᐱᑎᖃᐳᕝᒎᕝᓯᖅᖃ ᓄᑕᕝᓘᕝᓂᒎᒃ ᖃᖃᓪᓕᒥᒎᒃ ᑲᓇᑕᑉ ᑲᓇᕝᒎᕝᓕᑕ ᐅᑭᐳᖅᑯᖅᒎᕝᓘᒎᓂ.

ᖅᐱᖅᑖᓄᒃ.

Baffin Island.

Île de Baffin.

ᑭᓇᒡᕆᑦ ᑲᒥᓯᐱᐊᓗ ᐃᖃᓗᐃᑦ ᑕᑎᐅᕐᕈᐊᖢᓂᖕ.

Mountains and fiords on Frobisher Bay.

Montagnes et fjords de la baie Frobisher.

ᖃᐅᔪᖅᑐᖅ ᐅᔭᕋᕐᓯᑎᐅᖃᑕᖅ.

Winter majesty.

Majesté hivernale.

ᐅᓚᑦᑐᖅ ᐅᑰᑕᒃᔪᑦ, ᑕᓯᐅᕐᓴᐸᑦ.

High tide in winter, Frobisher Bay.

Marée haute en hiver, baie Frobisher.

18

ᐃᑦᑑᓯᓄᑦ ᖁᐊᖅᐊᐅᕐᓂᖁᖕᑕᖅᐳᖅ ᐃᓄᐃᑦ ᑕᒻᖏᐱᖃᑦᑎᖅᔭᐸᓂᖕᓂᖓ.

Archeological work continues on traditional Inuit camp sites.

Les fouilles archéologiques se poursuivent sur les sites de campement inuits traditionnels.

ᖃᒻᒪᐅᑦ ᐊᖅᑭᖅᔭᖓᑎᒪᓂᐅᑖᑕᖕᒻᖒ, ᕼᐊᓚᒍᖕᖓᒐᑐᖕᓄᑦ ᐊᖕᔪᓄᖑᑦ ᐃᓄᐃᑦ ᖃᑦᒫᖒ.

Typical framework of a *qarmaq*, a centuries-old Inuit sodhouse.

Structure typique d'une *qarmaq*, hutte de terre inuite centenaire.

ᐃᖃᓗᐃᑦ ᓯᓇ ᒦᓇ ᐊᑐᖅᑕᐅᔪᑦ ᐅᑭᐅᒃᑯᑦ ᐆᑦᑲᑐᓄᑦ.

The snowhouse is still used today during winter travel.

Les abris de glace sont toujours utilisés de nos jours durant les déplacements en hiver.

ᐃᓗᕖᑦ ᕗᕿᓐᓛᓐ ᐃᓚᒥᓚᐅᕐᑕᖏᓐᓄ ᐃᓅᔫᓐᓅᕐᓂᑯᑦ ᓅᖕᖑᕕᖕᒥᑦ ᖃᐅᓯᐃᑦᑑᑉ ᖃᓂᒌᔭᓂᑦ 1845–46.

The graves of Franklin's men who died at Beechey Island near Resolute Bay, 1845–46.

Sépulcre des hommes de Franklin morts à l'île Beechey, près de Resolute Bay, 1845–46.

ᓯᐅᑦᓕᖅᐸᖁᒻᒍᓄᑏᑉ ᒐᓇᐅᑉ ᐊᑭᐊᓂᐅᒻᓰᖅᓯᔭᕐᑕ ᐊᒃᖃᕐᓯᓚᕐᒍᑕ ᐅᑭᐅᖅᑕᖅᑐᒥ: ᑕᓕᕐᑕᒻᖁᓄ ᐅᐃᕐᓂᖁᔾᒍᒍ: ᐊᕐᓄᖅᖁᐅᖁᓐᒃᖁᑕᒃ, ᓂᐅᐃᖅᓐᑉᐅᑕᒃ, ᐅᐱᕐᓯᔭᑐᑯᓭᓐ ᐃᓪᓂᓄᑐᑯᐱᓐᖁᓭᓐ ᐊᔨᑲᐅᑐᓯᓂᓐᓐ, ᐸᓂᒻᖁᑕᒃ.

The faces of early European influence in the North: (clockwise) Anglican Mission, Hudson's Bay Company post, Roman Catholic Student Residence, RCMP detachment.

Les tributs de l'influence européenne initiale dans le Nord : (sens horaire) Mission anglicane, poste de la Compagnie de la Baie d'Hudson, résidence étudiante catholique romaine, détachement de la GRC.

ᐅᑭᐅᖅᑯᑦ ᐅᓐᓄᒃᓵᕆᑉᐸᖅᑐᖅ ᐅᑭᐅᕐᑐᒥᓐ.

Winter evenings come early North of Sixty.

En hiver, le soleil se couche tôt au nord du 60e parallèle.

ᐊᐅᔭᑎᓐᓲᒍ ᐊᐱᑐᖅᓯᓚᓂᐊᑕ ᐊᖕᔨᖅᖃᖅᐱᐊᖕᓂ.

Summer view of the territorial capital.

La capitale territoriale en été.

ᓄᓇᓖᑦ ᖃᓄᐃᓕᐅᖅᑐᖏᑦ

Community idiosyncracies!

Idiosyncrasies communautaires !

ᖃᑉᓗᓈᖅᑐᑦ ᐃᓄᖏᑦᑎᒃᓴᐅᑎᐱᓄᒐᖕᖓᑦ ᓂᐊᖅᐃᓐᓂᒪᒐᓂᒃᑯ.

The original Hudson's Bay Company buildings in Apex.

Les édifices originaux de la Compagnie de la Baie d'Hudson à Apex.

ᓂᐊᖅᐃᓐᓂᒪᒐ, ᓄᓇᓕᑦ 5 ᑭᓚᒥᑦᕐᓂ ᐅᖃᓕᕐᓂᒐᓂᒃ ᐃᖃᓗᕐᓂᒃᑦ.

Apex, a small community five kilometres from Iqaluit.

Apex, une petite localité à cinq kilomètres d'Iqaluit.

ᒥᑦᑕᕝ ᓴᓇᔪᐊᖅᓚᒃᐅᑐᖅᓂᖔᖅ ᐊᒥᐊᓕᑲᑦ ᐅᓇᑕᖅᑎᖑᔾᔭᖓᓄᑦ 1942-ᒥ.

The first airstrip was built by the American military in 1942.

La première base aérienne construite par les forces militaires américaines en 1942.

ᐅᐊᑕᖅᖅᐹᔫᑦ ᖃᖑᑕᔪᐱᓐᑦ ᓯᓀ ᐊᐅᑕᐸᐸᔫᑦ ᖅᑭᖅᖕᑖᓯᒥ.

Military aircraft continue to operate in the Baffin region.

Les avions militaires continuent à parcourir la région de Baffin.

ᒪᖕᓇ ᓯᖅᖅᑎᖅᖅᑕᐸᔭᒪᔪᖅ, ᓄᐊᕝᑯᖕᒥᔪᐸᐊᑎᑦᓯᖅ ᖅᖅᐳᑦᑕᐸᔭᖅᔪᖅ ᐃᓚᖕᒃᔪᑦ ᐅᐊᑕᑐᖅᖅᔪᑦ ᐊᓂ°ᐱᐃᓂᑐᖅᖕᓂᓛ ᓇᕐᐱᔭᒥᓄᓇ 1950-ᖕᒥᓂ.

Now demolished, Upper Base formed part of the Distant Early Warning Line built in the 1950s.

Aujourd'hui démolie, la Upper Base formait une partie de la ligne de Détection lointaine avancée construite dans les années 1950.

ᐅᓇᒌ ᔅᑯᓯᐅᕝᖓᖁ ᓂᑭᑐᑕ ᒪᐃᐊᔅᖁᔪᑐᓯᑎᖅ ᐅᒌᐊᔭᐊᑕᐅᖃᒿᕝᐊᓄᓗᕋᐸᓗᑎ.

The Canadian Coastguard arrives to open the shipping season.

La Garde côtière canadienne arrive pour l'ouverture de la saison de la navigation.

ᐃᖃᓗᓐᓂ ᐅᒋᐊᕐᐊᖅ ᐊᐅᔭᕆᓕ ᓂᑭᐸᑲᖅ ᓄᑲᖃᓄᕐᒉᕝᖃᑕᐅᖅᐸᖑᐊᖏᓐᓗᒍ ᑲᓇᒋᐊ.

The Iqaluit "sealift" takes place each summer despite some of the largest tides in Canada.

Le transport maritime se fait chaque été à Iqaluit, en dépit des plus fortes marées au Canada.

ᐃᓗᐊᐱᐅᒃᑐᖅᑎᐅᑦ ᐊᖅᐱᖅᓯᒪᔪᖅ ᐃᖏᕐᓴᐊᑐᖅ ᐊᑎᐅᑦ ᑐᑉᐊᖅᐸᔪᓐ, ᐊᑭᑐᒎᒃ ᓯᓚᐅᑉᓯᒪᔪᖅ 2005-ᖕᒍᑎᓐᓜᒎ.

The igloo-shaped St.Jude's Anglican cathedral, destroyed by fire in 2005.

La cathédrale anglicane Saint-Jude, en forme d'igloo, détruite par le feu en 2005.

ᑐᒃᕕᐊᖕᔪᐊᑦ ᐃᓅᐊᓄ ᑕᑯᒃᐸᓄᖅᑎᖁᕐᒪᔪᖅ ᐃᓄᐃᑦ ᐃᓚᒃᕝᐊᑐᖅᑲᓄᒌᖕᓄᒃ.

The cathedral's interior reflected Inuit traditions.

L'intérieur de la cathédrale, évoqué dans l'art traditionnel inuit.

ᐊᕐᕿᒍᑕᓖᓐ ᐊᑐᕐᑕᐅᕙᒃᑐᖅ ᓱᑲᓐᓂᕈᓯᐅᑎᓂᖅ ᐃᖃᓗᓐᓂᑦ ᑭᒻᒥᕈᒻᒧᑦ ᑐᓂᖅ ᑕᐃᒻᒥᓐ.

The annual Iqaluit–Kimmirut snowmobile race at Toonik Tyme.

La course annuelle Iqaluit–Kimmirut en motoneige à l’occasion du Toonik Tyme.

ᑐᓂᖅ ᑕᐃᒻ.

Toonik Tyme.

Toonik Tyme.

"ᖃᖑᒡᓗᑦᑕᕈᖅ."

"The airplane."

« L'avion ».

ᐊᐱᕐᓱᖅ, ᓯᐳᑦᑎᖕ ᐊᒍᑐᑕᑕᑎ.

String games, a link with the past.

Les jeux de ficelles – un lien avec le passé.

ᖁᓪᓕᖅ, ᐃᓄᐃᑦ ᐊᑐᖅᑲᑕᖅᑕᖓ ᐅᖅᔪᖅᑐᐱᐅᒋ ᖃᐅᒪᓕᖕᓄ.

The *Qulliq*, the traditional Inuit source of heat and light.

Le *qulliq*, une source d'éclairage et de chauffage inuite traditionnelle.

ᐃᐱᔪᓯᓄᑦ ᓴᓇᕐᑐᑕᓕᐊᑦ ᓄᓂᐊᕐᑕᒥᐅᓄᑦ.

Grass baskets from Sanikiluaq.

Paniers de paille de Sanikiluaq.

ᓇᕐᑐᐊᓕᑦ, ᐱᒪᓐᐅᖃᑕᐅᔪᑦ ᑌᑭᐅᑦᐸᑐᒥ ᐱᕙᓪᓕᐊᓂᓗ.

Carving, an important part of the northern economy.

La sculpture, élément important de l'économie dans le Nord.

ᑎᑎᕐᑐᒐᕐᑕᐅᕆᓪᓕᒃ ᑮᓈᓕᑦ ᑎᑎᕐᑐᓕᕐᕕᒻᒥᓂ ᑮᓈᓗᓯᓐ.

Print-making at Kinngait Studios in Cape Dorset.

Production de gravures aux studios Kinngait Studios, à Cape Dorset.

ᐧᑭᓯᓂ ᓲᒪᖅᓴᐅᐨ.

Cleaning sealskins.

Apprêtage de peaux de phoque.

ᐊᑭᓈᑕᑕᐅᐧᑐᑦ ᐅᖅᒥᑕ ᒥᔅᖅᐱᓄᓄᑦ ᐸᙱᕐᑐᖅ.

Tapestry-making at the Uqqurmiut Centre in Pangnirtung.

Tapisserie au centre Uqqurmiut, à Pangnirtung.

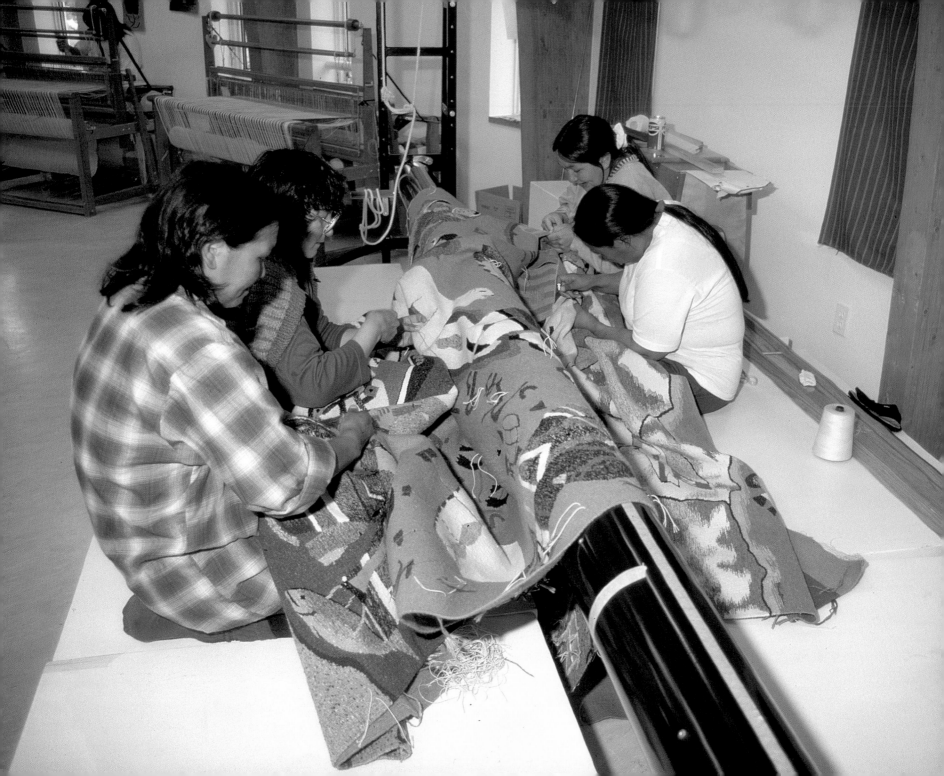

ᐃᓄᐃᑦ ᕿᒧᒃᓯᕐᓂᐅᑎᖏᑦ, ᓱᓕ ᐃᓚᒋᔭᐅᒻᒪᕆᒃᐳᑦ ᐅᑭᐅᖅᑕᖅᑐᒥ ᐃᓅᓯᕆᔭᐅᔪᓂ.

The Inuit sled dog, still a part of northern life.

Le chien de traîneau fait encore partie de la vie nordique.

ᕿᒧᒃᓯᕐᓂᖅ ᐊᑐᖃᑦᑕᕐᑐᖅ ᓱᓕ.

The dogteam tradition continues.

La tradition des équipes de chiens se poursuit.

ᐊᖓᔪᖅᑐᖅ ᓄᕐᕈᐊᐃᑦ ᖃᓂᒌᔪᓂᖅ.

Hunting near Qikiqtarjuaq.

La chasse près de Qikiqtarjuaq.

ᖁᒧᔪᐊᖅᑐᖅ, ᐅᑭᐅᑕᖅᑐᒥ ᐊᑐᕐᑕᐅᒃᑐᖅ.

Adventure by dogteam, an Arctic experience.

Une excursion en traîneau à chiens – une expérience unique à l'Arctique.

ᒪᐅᔭᕐᔪᑏᑦ.

Ice-pan hopping.

Les sauts en radeau de glace.

ᐊᐅᓚᓱᖅ ᑕᓯᒪᐅᑕᒥ.

Jigging for cod.

La pêche à la morue au jig.

ᒥᑭᒥᐊᕐᓂᖅ, ᐃᓅᓯᕐᒧᓐ ᐃᑲᔫᑎᐅᒐᓗᐊᖅ ᑭᓯᐊᓂ ᐊᒃᓯᕿᕐᓇᕐᑐᖅ.

Trapping, no easy way to make a living.

Le trappage – un moyen bien dur de gagner sa vie.

ᐃᓕᖅᑯᓯᑐᖃᑎᒍᑦ ᑐᒃᑑᑉ ᐊᒥᖓᓂ ᐊᒪᐅᑎ.

The traditional caribou-skin *amautik*.

L'amautik – traditionellement fait de peau de caribou.

ᑐᒃᑐ, ᐱᒪᓇᐅᔭᖅ ᓂᕿᐅᔭᓐᓂᖃᕐᓂᓗᑦ ᐊᓐᓄᕋᔭᓐᓂᖃᕐᓂᓗᑎᓪ.

Caribou, an important source of food and clothing.

Le caribou, une source d'aliments et de vêtements importante.

ᑎᕆᓕᐊᕐᔪᑦ ᓱᓕ ᑕᐅᑐᒃᑕᐅᔪᑦ ᓄᓇᕗᑦ ᓄᓇᓕᓐᓂᑦ ᖃᓂᒋᔭᖏᓐᓂ.

Foxes can still be seen near many Nunavut communities.

Le renard habite toujours à proximité des localités du Nunavut.

ᐅᒥᖕᒪᒃ ᐊᐅᔭᐃᑦᐅᑦ ᖃᓐᖐᖃᓂᓂ.

Muskoxen near Grise Fiord.

Boeufs musqués près de Grise Fiord.

ᓄᓇᖅ ᐊᖑᔭᕆᓂᒃ ᐸᖅᑭᔭᖅᓯᒪᖅ.

Young bear protecting a kill.

Un jeune ours protégeant sa prise.

ᐃᓄᐃᑦ, ᑐᓗᒑᖕᑐᖅ ᓄᐊᴿᐊᖕᑐᓄ ᔅᒡᖕ ᐅᓄᐊᑕᓛᒡ.

Living off the land.

Aux frais de la couronne.

ᐃᒥᖅᑕᐃᓐᓇᖅ, ᐅᖃᖠᖅᑐᒥᖕᓂᓄ ᐊᐅᔭᑕᓐ ᐅᑭᐅᖅᑕᖅᑐᒥᔾᖅ.

The arctic tern, an annual long-distance summer visitor.

La sterne arctique – un visiteur annuel qui vient de loin.

ᓇᐅᔭᖅ (ᓇᐅᔭᔅᑲᖅ).

Ivory Gulls.

Mouettes blanches.

ᖃᔭᖅ, ᐃᓄᐃᑦ ᐊᒡᒋᕐᓂᖁᓕ ᓴᖅᑭᔪᐊᖅ.

The *kayak*, Inuit ingenuity at its best.

Le *kayak* – modèle de l'ingéniosité inuite.

ᐊᬟᖓᎠᑎ ᐅᒥᐊᖅ ᕿᑭᖅᑕᖅᔪᐊᕐᒥ.

Whaling boat at Qikiqtarjuaq.

Baleinier à Qikiqtarjuaq.

ᓄᓇᕗᑦ ᓄᓇᓕᖏᑦ (ᑕᐃᒃᓴᐱᐊᖓᓄᑦ ᓴᐅᒥᖓᓄᑦ (ᑭᖓᓂᖅᐸᓂᐅᑉ ᐃᕐᖓᖅᓯᓇᖅᑕᐅᑎᑕᖓ): ᐃᒃᐱᐊᕐᔪᒃ, ᐊᐅᓯᐃᑦᑐᖅ, ᑕᓗᕐᔪᐊᖅ, ᕿᑭᖅᑕᕐᔪᐊᖅ.

Nunavut communities (clockwise): Arctic Bay, Grise Fiord, Taloyoak, Qikiqtarjuaq.

Communautés du Nunavut (sens horaire) : Arctic Bay, Grise Fiord, Taloyoak, Qikiqtarjuaq.

ᐸᖕᓂᕐᑐᖅ, ᐊᐅᓯᐅᑦᑐᖅ ᒥᕐᖑᐃᓯᖃᕐᕕᐅᑉ ᐹᓂᑦ.

Pangnirtung, near the southern entrance to Auyuittuq National Park.

Pangnirtung, près de l'entrée sud du parc national Auyuittuq.

ᐊᐅᔭᐃᑦᑐᖅ ᒥᕐᖑᐃᓯᕐᕕᕻ.

Auyuittuq National Park.

Parc national Auyuittuq.

ᖁᕕᐊᓱᓐᓂᖅ ᐅᑭᐅᒃᑕᖅᑐᒥ ᖁᖏᓂᖅᑯᑦ!

Happiness is a northern smile!

Le bonheur, un sourire nordique!

ᐱᓂᐊᐅᑎᐿᑐᑦ ᐱᕐᖃᑎᓄᖕᓂᖅ.

The next generation of providers.

La prochaine génération de fournisseurs.

ᓄᓇᕗᒻᒥᐅᑦ – ᐱᖁᓕᒫᖅᑑᑎᒋᓪᓗᒍ!

Nunavummiut – and proud of it!

Nunavummiut – et fier de l'être!

ᑲᓇᑕᖅᑐᒃᖕᖕᒍᑎᒃ ᐱᓕᕆᑎᓪᓗᒋᑦ ᓴᓂᑭᓗᐊᕐᒥ.

Canadian Rangers on duty in Sanikiluaq.

Gardes canadiens en devoir à Sanikiluaq.

ᓯᕗᓪᓕᖅᐹᒥᑦ ᑲᑎᒪᓂᕆᔾᔪᑦ ᓄᓇᕗᑦ ᒪᓕᒐᓕᐅᕐᕕᖓᓂ, 1 ᐃᐳᕆ 1999.

First sitting of the Legislative Assembly of Nunavut, 1 April 1999.

Première séance de l'Assemblée législative du Nunavut, le 1er avril 1999.

ᐊᔾᔨᙳᐊᑦ 1999-ᒥ ᓄᓇᕗᑖᖅᑎᓪᓗᒋᑦ ᓇᓪᓕᐅᓂᖅᓯᐅᕈᑎᖃᖅᑐᑦ: (ᓯᕿᙵᔪᐃᑉ ᐃᖏᕐᕋᓂᔾᔪᖕᖓᑎᑦ) ᓄᓇᕗᒥ ᐊᓐᓄᕋᓂᒃᓴᐅᑉᐳᑦ, ᒐᕙᒪᓕᕆᓂᕐᒧᑦ ᓯᕗᓪᓕᖅᑎᐅᓯᒪᔪᑦ, ᐃᓄᐃᑦ ᑲᑐᔾᔨᖃᑎᒌᖕᒋᑦ, ᐊᕕᒃᑐᖅᓯᒪᓂᐊᓂ ᓴᐃᒻᒪᑎᖓᑦ.

Scenes from the 1999 creation of Nunavut celebrations: (clockwise) Nunavut fashion, Political pioneers, The People's Party, The territorial flag.

Scènes des célébrations de la création du Nunavut, en 1999 : (sens horaire) La mode au Nunavut, politiciens pionniers, le parti du peuple, le drapeau territorial.

ᓯᕐᕿᓂᖅ ᐳᐃᒃᑐᖅ.

Sun mirages, part of the mystique of the Arctic.

Les mirages, élément mystique de l'Arctique.

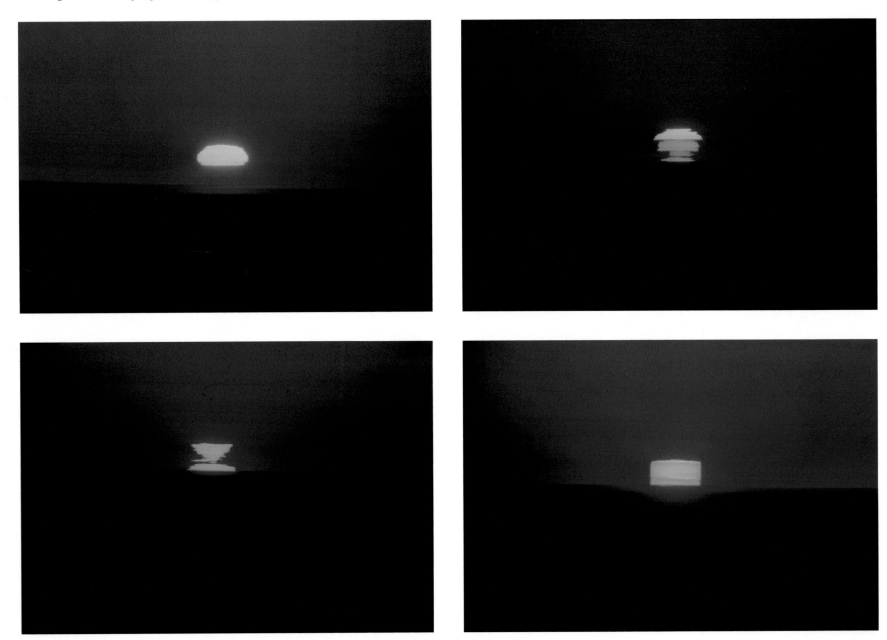

ᓯᕐᑭᓂᖅ ᑕᕐᕋᓚᒃ ᐃᒫᒎᓐᓂ, ᐅᑭᐅᑦᑕᖅᑐᒥ ᑕᑯᒃᓴᐅᔫᖅ.

Sun-dogs, a common northern phenomenon.

Les faux soleils, un phénomène propre à l'Arctique.

ᐃᓄᒃᓱᒃᑲᖅ, ᐅᑭᐅᕆᑕᖅᑐᒥ ᓇᓗᓇᐃᒃᑯᑎ.

The *inuksuk,* landmark of the North.

L'*inuksuk,* un point de repère dans le Nord.